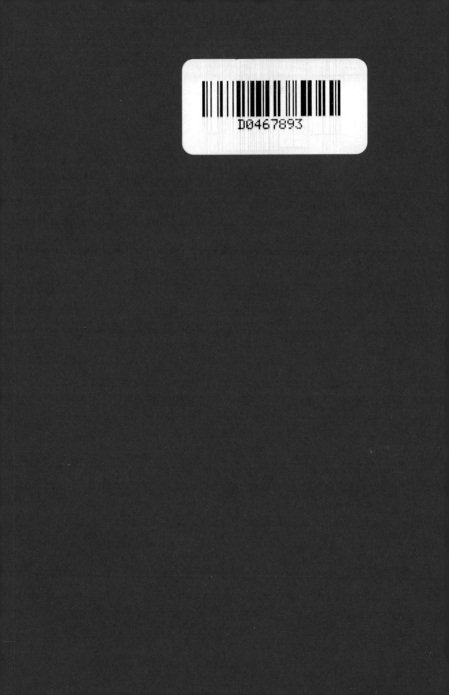

THE BUDDHA IS STILL TEACHING

ALSO BY JACK KORNFIELD

After the Ecstasy, the Laundry

The Art of Forgiveness, Lovingkindness and Peace

The Buddha's Little Instruction Book

Living Dharma

Meditation for Beginners

A Path With Heart

Seeking the Heart of Wisdom (with Joseph Goldstein)

Soul Food (with Christina Feldman)

A Still Forest Pool (with Paul Breiter)

Teachings of the Buddha

The Wise Heart

THE BUDDHA
IS STILL TEACHING

CONTEMPORARY BUDDHIST WISDOM

selected and edited by

JACK KORNFIELD

With Noelle Oxenhandler

SHAMBHALA
BOSTON AND LONDON
2010

Shambhala Publications, Inc.
Horticultural Hall
300 Massachusetts Avenue
Boston, Massachusetts 02115
www.shambhala.com

Cover art: Standing Buddha, 15th century. Thailand,
Lan Na style. Gilt bronze, H. 61^1/$_2$ in. (156.2 cm).
Gift of Cynthia Hazen Polsky, 191 (191.423.5).
May have restrictions. Image copyright
© The Metropolitan Museum of Art/Art Resource, N.Y.
The Metropolitan Museum of Art, New York, N.Y. U.S.A.
D00094466. ART403907.

9 8 7 6 5 4 3 2 1

First Edition
Printed in the United States of America

⊗This edition is printed on acid-free paper that meets the
American National Standards Institute Z39.48 Standard.
♻This book was printed on 30% postconsumer
recycled paper. For more information please visit
www.shambhala.com.

Distributed in the United States by Random House, Inc.,
and in Canada by Random House of Canada Ltd

Dedicated

to the generation of teachers

who have so beautifully carried

the lamp of the Dharma

to the West.

CONTENTS

—

A collection of meditation practices to accompany this book
is available for free at www.shambhala.com/still teaching.

INTRODUCTION
BY JACK KORNFIELD

You hold in your hands a modern treasure, the equivalent of new Buddhist sutras. These are the words of awakening from contemporary masters. The teachings of the Buddha are called the Lion's Roar, words of fearlessness and unshakable freedom. On the night of his enlightenment, the Buddha awakened to the vast and timeless peace of nirvana. He proclaimed that the ropes of clinging and sorrow were snapped, the clouds of confusion and fear dissipated, the powers of aggression and doubt were defeated. He was silently and joyfully free.

For forty-five years afterward, he wandered the dusty roads of India proclaiming this freedom and teaching the path of wisdom and compassion to all who had ears to hear. These teachings were eventually written down as sutras, careful records of the teachings of Buddha. These traditional texts include his instructions, his dialogues with students, and accounts of his words pointing the way to liberation. The earliest sutras date from more than twenty-five hundred years ago, while others are teachings from the Buddha Mind written down by enlightened disciples in subsequent centuries.

The words of the Buddha have great power. The ancient stories tell of many who became enlightened simply by hearing him speak. Ananda, the Buddha's attendant, has depicted these teaching scenes for us, describing how the monks and nuns were seated at the cool wood of Tapoda or in Jivaka's mango grove, or how a thousand followers were gathered at Vultures Peak. As they listened to the Buddha, their hearts were freed from entanglement in the changing conditions of the world. Their understanding shifted from a limited sense of self, caught in the illusion of separateness and clinging, to the peace of nirvana, open and free. They tasted the joyful freedom experienced when clinging, hatred, and ignorance drop away. Each time he taught, the Buddha pointed the way to this timeless freedom.

In the same way, the freedom taught by the Buddha is brought to life by the teachers of awakening in modern times. When Zen Master Suzuki Roshi first gave teachings on beginner's mind, the hearts of many of the students listening were opened to a freedom beyond past and future. When the Dalai Lama took the teaching seat surrounded by thousands of followers in New York's Madison Square Garden, he pointed the way to the same liberation and compassion as the Buddha. When Sharon Salzberg and Pema Chödrön speak to crowds of students on loving-kindness and compassion, the human suffering of all who listen, their conflicts and judgment, are all held in a vast spaciousness of freedom that is our true nature.

These are the words you will find in this book. What makes these modern teachings authentic is the understanding that the true Buddha is not limited to the body or mind of a particular man who lived long ago. The Buddha himself explained this. In the ancient sutras, there is a story of a devoted young monk who was so enraptured that he spent weeks sitting at the feet of the Buddha, simply gazing reverently at him as he taught. Finally the Buddha chastised him, saying, "You do not even see me. To see the Buddha, you must see the Dharma, the truth. One who sees the Dharma sees me."

In these pages, you will find the Dharma. Dharma means both truth and the path to discover the truth. The Dharma is kept alive by all who follow the path. In the forest monasteries of Asia, just before the dawn, the monks and nuns gather in the Buddha Hall to meditate and to chant "*ehipasiko, opanaiko, paccattang veditabbho vinuhittii.*" The Dharma of liberation is "immediate, open-handed, timeless, visible to the wise, to be experienced here and now by each person in their own heart." In every generation, this invitation is repeated in an unbroken lineage of voices, a call to live with the great freedom of a Buddha and to discover for yourself the path of virtue, compassion, and wisdom. These teachings are an invitation to the death less, to timeless freedom amid the changing seasons of the world.

The Buddha insisted that his awakened disciples, when traveling to new lands, teach the Dharma in the language and vernacular of their times. In this book, you will find this instruction fulfilled in the voices of seventy-five contemporary teachers—male and female, old and young, from each of the great contemplative traditions of Buddhism. Of course, the task of selection was a difficult one. For every Dharma gem that found its way into this book, a thousand more are sparkling in the Dharma books of our time. Among the gems that did find their way into this collection, you will find words from Kalu Rinpoche that illuminate the emptiness of all things, poems by Thich Nhat Hanh that express our profound interdependence, and teachings that invite your awakened heart to grow in loving-kindness, compassion, equanimity, and joy.

The presentation of these texts begins with teachers who focus on right understanding and mindfulness, then moves on to the heart of compassion and forgiveness. Next are ways to work with obstacles, and illuminated passages on impermanence, healing, death, emptiness, karma, and liberation. The teachings conclude with Dharma in daily life, engaged Buddhism, and a pair of foundational meditation practices. In this simple volume, you will find beautiful invocations of generosity; celebrations of courage; and practices to quiet the mind, transform difficulties, and liberate the spirit. You will even find some words spoken by Gandhi and Martin Luther King Jr. that echo those of the Buddha.

These teachings are the good medicine of the Dharma. Read them slowly, listen to them. Let these luminous words bring the Buddha's awakening to your own heart and mind. Reflect on them, practice them, let them transform your life.

These words will bless you.

For these are the teachings that are
good in the beginning,
good in the middle, and good in the end.

May you be joyful and free.

Jack Kornfield
Spirit Rock Center
Woodacre, California
2010

WISE UNDERSTANDING

ILLUSION AND REALITY

You live in illusion and the appearance of things.
There is a reality, but you do not know this.
When you understand this, you will see that
you are nothing.
And being nothing, you are everything.
That is all.

—Kalu Rinpoche,
The Dharma: That Illuminates All Beings Impartially
Like the Light of the Sun and the Moon

YOUR OWN PSYCHOLOGIST

To become your own psychologist, you don't have to learn some big philosophy. All you have to do is examine your own mind every day. You already examine material things every day—every morning you check out the food in your kitchen—but you never investigate your mind. Checking your mind is much more important.

—Lama Yeshe,
*Becoming Your Own Therapist and
Making Your Mind an Ocean*

BEGINNER'S MIND

People say that practicing Zen is difficult, but there is a misunderstanding as to why. It is not difficult because it is hard to sit in the cross-legged position, or to attain enlightenment. It is difficult because it is hard to keep our mind pure and our practice pure in its fundamental sense. . . .

In Japan we have the phrase *shoshin,* which means "beginner's mind." The goal of practice is always to keep our beginner's mind. Suppose you recite the Prajna Paramita Sutra only once. It might be a very good recitation. But what would happen to you if you recited it twice, three times, four times, or more? You might easily lose your original attitude towards it. The same thing will happen in your other Zen practices. For a while you keep your beginner's mind, but if you continue to practice one, two, three years or more, although you may improve some, you are liable to lose the limitless meaning of original mind.

For Zen students the most important thing is not to be dualistic. Our "original mind" includes everything within itself. It is always rich and sufficient within itself. You should not lose your self-sufficient state of mind. This does not mean a closed mind, but actually an empty mind and a ready mind. If your mind is empty, it is always ready for anything; it is open to everything. In the beginner's mind, there are many possibilities; in the expert's mind, there are few.

—Shunryu Suzuki, *Zen Mind, Beginner's Mind*

A STILL FOREST POOL

Try to be mindful and let things take their natural course. Then your mind will become still in any surroundings, like a clear forest pool. All kinds of wonderful, rare animals will come to drink at the pool, and you will clearly see the nature of all things. You will see many strange and wonderful things come and go, but you will be still. This is the happiness of the Buddha.

—Ajahn Chah in *A Still Forest Pool:*
The Insight Meditation of Achaan Chah,
by Jack Kornfield and Paul Breiter

THE ART OF LIVING

The art of living . . . is neither careless drifting on the one hand nor fearful clinging to the past . . . on the other. It consists in being sensitive to each moment, in regarding it as utterly new and unique, in having the mind open and wholly receptive.

—Alan Watts, *The Wisdom of Insecurity:*
A Message for an Age of Anxiety

WHERE IS HAPPINESS

In 1979 I decided to become a nun. Up until that time, I had tried a lot of things and had seen that the world cannot make one happy. In the course of [these] travels it became clear to me that tranquility and peace have nothing to do with the most beautiful places on earth or the most interesting experiences. They are only to be found in one's own heart.

—Ayya Khema, *I Give You My Life:*
The Autobiography of a Western Buddhist Nun

A PATH WITH HEART

In undertaking a spiritual life, what matters is simple: *We must make certain that ours is a path with heart.* Many other visions are offered to us in the modern spiritual marketplace. Spiritual traditions offer stories of enlightenment, bliss, knowledge, divine ecstasy, and the highest possibilities of the human spirit. Out of the broad range of teachings available to us in the world, often we are first attracted to these glamorous and most extraordinary aspects. While the promise of attaining such states can come true, and while these states do represent the teachings in one sense, they are also one of the advertising techniques of the spiritual trade. They are not the goal of spiritual life.

In the end, spiritual life is not a process of seeking or gaining some extraordinary condition or special powers. In fact, such seeking can take us away from ourselves and from awakening. If we are not careful, we can easily find the great failures of our modern society—its ambitions, materialism, and individual isolation—repeated in our spiritual life.

In beginning a genuine spiritual journey, we have to stay much closer to home, to focus directly on what is right here in front of us, to make sure that our path is connected with love and a simple, compassionate presence. Listening with the heart to the mystery here and now is where meditation begins.

—Jack Kornfield, adapted from *A Path With Heart: A Guide through the Perils and Promises of Spiritual Life*

REALIZE WHERE YOU ARE

Meditation is the only intentional, systematic human activity which at bottom is about *not* trying to improve yourself or get anywhere else, but simply to realize where you already are. Perhaps its value lies precisely in this. Maybe we all need to do one thing in our lives simply for its own sake.

—Jon Kabat-Zinn, *Wherever You Go, There You Are: Mindfulness Meditation in Everyday Life*

SPIRITUAL MATERIALISM

According to the Buddhist tradition, the spiritual path is the process of cutting through our confusion, of uncovering the awakened state of mind. When the awakened state of mind is crowded in by ego and its attendant paranoia, it takes on the character of an underlying instinct. So it is not a matter of building up the awakened state of mind, but rather of burning out the confusions which obstruct it. In the process of burning out these confusions, we discover enlightenment. If the process were otherwise, the awakened state of mind would be a product, dependent upon cause and effect and therefore liable to dissolution. Anything which is created must, sooner or later, die. If enlightenment were created in such a way, there would always be the possibility of ego reasserting itself, causing a return to the confused state. Enlightenment is permanent because we have not produced it; we have merely discovered it. In the Buddhist tradition, the analogy of the sun appearing from behind the clouds is often used to explain the discovery of enlightenment.

· · ·

We have come here to learn about spirituality. I trust the genuine quality of this search but we must question its nature. The problem is that ego can convert anything to its own use, even spirituality . . . if our teacher speaks of renunciation of ego, we attempt to mimic renunciation of ego. We go through the motions, make the appropriate gestures, but we really do not want to sacrifice any part of our way of life. . . .

It is important to see that the main point of any spiritual practice is to step out of the bureaucracy of ego. This means stepping out of ego's constant desire for a higher, more spiritual, more transcendental version of knowledge, religion, virtue, judgment, comfort, or whatever it is that the particular ego is seeking. One must step out of spiritual materialism.

—Chögyam Trungpa, *Cutting Through Spiritual Materialism*

ALTOGETHER ONE LIFE

So we ask, what are we? What is our unchanging essence? What we think we are, unfortunately, is not what we are, or at most only a very small portion of it. A large amount can't be contained in a small container. Our life is like an iceberg; we can consciously perceive only a small portion of it. The larger portion is under water. If we try to understand our life using our limited knowledge, understanding is impossible. What is our life? As Buddha and all the masters tell us, it's altogether one life. Even saying "one" sounds silly. Since everything is nothing but your life, it's quite all right that some things are big and some are small, some are high and some are low, some are dark and some are light. But since we find it difficult to accept things as they are, we have to practice, and the struggle begins.

—Taizan Maezumi in *The Hazy Moon of Enlightenment: Part of the On Zen Practice Collection*, by Taizan Maezumi and Bernie Glassman

FIRST, SEE HOW IT IS

To practice, we must start exactly where we are. Of course, we can always imagine perfect conditions, how it should be ideally, how everyone else should behave. But it's not our task to create an ideal. It's our task to see how it is and to learn from the world as it is. For the awakening of the heart, conditions are always good enough.

—Ajahn Sumedho, *The Way It Is*

NOT BY BREAD ALONE

The pursuit of real happiness. What do we mean by that? That we do not live by bread alone. That all our opportunity will be stultifying and boring if we do not know what makes us happy and how to pursue it. That happiness should be ours, and there are methods for discovering which happiness is really reliable and satisfying, and then securing that in an enduring way without depriving others.

—Robert Thurman, *Inner Revolution: Life, Liberty, and the Pursuit of Real Happiness*

REBELLION AND HAPPINESS

It has been my experience that rebelling against the forces of attachment within my own heart and mind has been the most revolutionary thing I've ever done.

We are addicted to pleasure, in part because we confuse pleasure with happiness. We would all say that deep down, all we want is to be happy. Yet we don't have a realistic understanding of what happiness really is. Happiness is closer to the experience of acceptance and contentment than it is to pleasure. True happiness exists as the spacious and compassionate heart's willingness to feel whatever is present.

—Noah Levine, *Against the Stream: A Buddhist Manual for Spiritual Revolutionaries*

BELONGING

When we are free of mental concepts and our senses are awake, the sounds, smells, images, and vibrations we experience connect us with all life everywhere. It is not *my* pain, it is the earth's pain. It is not my aliveness but simply life—unfolding and intense, mysterious and beautiful. By meeting the changing dance of sensation with Radical Acceptance, we discover our intrinsic belonging to this world. We are "no thing"—not limited to any passing experience—and "everything," belonging to the whole.

—Tara Brach, *Radical Acceptance*

EARTHRISE FROM THE MOON

My favorite photo is earthrise as seen from the moon. It's perfect. A great blue and green ball floating in vast black space, hanging right there in its orbit. From that vantage point, the scene on earth is awesome. Creatures being born, other ones dying; plants blooming on one side, plants withering on the other; snow snowing, winds blowing, volcanoes erupting, earthquakes shivering, people talking, music playing. From the moonview, it's incredible cosmic drama. From our usual view, inside the drama, looking up at the moon, it's a different story. It changes from *the* drama to *my* drama and gets to be a problem. If you're far enough away, it's not your story—it's one of the six and a half billion stories.

Remembering the two views SIMULTANEOUSLY is a great challenge.

—Sylvia Boorstein, *It's Easier Than You Think:*
The Buddhist Way to Happiness

THE BIRTH OF BODHICITTA

A young woman wrote to me about finding herself in a small town in the Middle East surrounded by people jeering, yelling, and threatening to throw stones at her and her friends because they were Americans. Of course, she was terrified, and what happened to her is interesting. Suddenly she identified with every person throughout history who had ever been scorned and hated. She understood what it was like to be despised for any reason: ethnic group, racial background, sexual preference, gender. Something cracked wide open, and she stood in the shoes of millions of oppressed people and saw with a new perspective. She even understood her shared humanity with those who hated her. This sense of deep connection, of belonging to the same family, is bodhichitta.

—Pema Chödrön, *The Places That Scare You:*
A Guide to Fearlessness in Difficult Times

WITHOUT FAITH

Those who do not have faith in others will not be able to stand on their own. Those who are always suspicious will be lonely.

—Sheng Yen, *Faith in Mind: A Commentary on Seng Ts'an's Classic*

THE BUTTERFLY OR THE COCOON

It's hard to know whether to laugh or to cry at the human predicament. Here we are with so much wisdom and tenderness, and—without even knowing it—we cover it over to protect ourselves from insecurity. Although we have the potential to experience the freedom of a butterfly, we mysteriously prefer the small and fearful cocoon of ego.

—Pema Chödrön, *The Places That Scare You:*
A Guide to Fearlessness in Difficult Times

WHIRLPOOLS IN THE RIVER

We are rather like whirlpools in the river of life. In flowing forward, a river or stream may hit rocks, branches, or irregularities in the ground, causing whirlpools to spring up spontaneously here and there. Water entering one whirlpool quickly passes through and rejoins the river, eventually joining another whirlpool and moving on. Though for short periods it seems to be distinguishable as a separate event, the water in the whirlpools is just the river itself. The stability of a whirlpool is only temporary. The energy of the river of life forms living things—a human being, a cat or dog, trees and plants—then what held the whirlpool in place is itself altered, and the whirlpool is swept away, reentering the larger flow. The energy that was a particular whirlpool fades out and the water passes on, perhaps to be caught again and turned for a moment into another whirlpool.

We'd rather not think of our lives in this way, however. We don't want to see ourselves as simply a temporary formation, a whirlpool in the river of life. The fact is, we take form for a while; then when conditions are appropriate, we fade out. There's nothing wrong with fading out; it's a natural part of the process. However, we want to think that this little whirlpool that we are isn't part of the stream. We want to see ourselves as permanent and stable. Our whole energy goes into trying to protect our supposed separateness. To protect the separateness, we set up artificial, fixed boundaries; as a consequence, we accumulate excess baggage, stuff that slips into our whirlpool and can't flow out again. So, things clog up our whirlpool and the process gets messy. The stream needs to flow naturally and freely. . . . We serve other whirlpools best if the water that enters ours is free to rush through and move on easily and quickly to whatever else needs to be stirred. The energy of life seeks rapid transformation. If we can see life this way and not cling to anything, life simply comes and goes.

—Charlotte Joko Beck, *Nothing Special: Living Zen*

CLING TO NAUGHT

There are many different descriptions of awakening, but all Buddhist traditions converge in one understanding of what liberates the mind. The Buddha expressed it clearly and unequivocally: "Nothing whatsoever is to be clung to as 'I' or 'mine.' Whoever has heard this truth has heard all the Teachings; whoever has realized this truth has realized all the Teachings." This is the essential unifying experience of freedom—the heart of the One Dharma of liberation. *Nothing whatsoever is to be clung to as "I" or "mine."*

—Joseph Goldstein, *One Dharma:*
The Emerging Western Buddhism

PLEASE CALL ME BY MY TRUE NAMES

Do not say that I'll depart tomorrow—
even today I am still arriving.

Look deeply: every second I am arriving
to be a bud on a Spring branch,
to be a tiny bird, with still-fragile wings,
learning to sing in my new nest,
to be a caterpillar in the heart of a flower,
to be a jewel hiding itself in a stone.

I still arrive, in order to laugh and to cry,
to fear and to hope,
the rhythm of my heart is the birth and death
of all that are alive.

I am a mayfly metamorphosing
on the surface of the river,
And I am the bird which, when Spring comes,
arrives in time to eat the mayfly.

I am a frog swimming happily
in the clear water of a pond.
And I am the grass-snake
that silently feeds itself on the frog.

I am the child in Uganda, all skin and bones,
my legs as thin as bamboo sticks.
And I am the arms merchant,
selling deadly weapons to Uganda.

I am the twelve-year-old girl,
refugee on a small boat,
who throws herself into the ocean
after being raped by a sea pirate.
And I am the pirate,
my heart not yet capable
of seeing and loving.

I am a member of the politburo,
with plenty of power in my hands.
And I am the man who has to pay his
"debt of blood" to my people
dying slowly in a forced labor camp.

My joy is like Spring, so warm
it makes flowers bloom all over the Earth.

My pain is like a river of tears,
so full it fills up the four oceans.

Please call me by my true names,
so I can hear all my cries and laughter at once,
so I can see that my joy and pain are one.

Please call me by my true names,
so I can wake up
and so the door of my heart can be left open,
the door of compassion.

—Thich Nhat Hanh, *Being Peace*

JOY IN THE WELFARE OF OTHERS

We should reflect upon and make serious efforts to dissolve our attitude that views ourselves and others as being separate and distinct. We have seen that insofar as the wish to gain happiness and to avoid suffering is concerned, there is no difference at all. The same is also true of our *natural right* to be happy; just as we have the right to enjoy happiness and freedom from suffering, all other living beings have the same natural right. So wherein lies the difference? The difference lies in the number of sentient beings involved. When we speak of the welfare of ourselves, we are speaking of the welfare of only one individual, whereas the welfare of others encompasses the well-being of an infinite number of beings. From that point of view, we can understand that others' welfare is much more important than our own.

If our own and others' welfare were totally unrelated and independent of one another, we could make a case for neglecting others' welfare. But that is not the case. I am always related to others and heavily dependent on them: while I am an ordinary person, while I am on the path, and also once I have achieved the resultant state. If we reflect along these lines, the importance of working for the benefit of others emerges naturally.

You should also examine whether, by remaining selfish and self-centered despite the validity of the above points, you can still achieve happiness and fulfill your desires. If that were the case, then pursuit of your selfish and self-centered habits would be a reasonable course of action. But it is not. The nature of our existence is such that we must depend on the cooperation and kindness of others for our survival. It is an observable fact that the more we take the welfare of others to heart and work for their benefit, the more benefit we attain for ourselves. You can see this fact for yourself. On the other hand, the more selfish and self-centered you remain, the more lonely and miserable you become. You can observe this fact for yourself.

Therefore, if you definitely want to work for your own benefit and welfare, . . . it is better to take into account the welfare of others and to regard their welfare as more important than your own. By contemplating these points, you will certainly be able to strengthen more and more your attitude of cherishing the well-being of others.

—The Dalai Lama, *The World of Tibetan Buddhism: An Overview of Its Philosophy and Practice*

YOU AND ME TOGETHER

Once when I was staying with friends in Colorado, I took one of my favorite horses, Rocky, on a trail ride through some back country. I had ridden Rocky before, mostly in the arena. He was very intelligent, but he didn't know how to walk a trail. This was a new situation. I was leading the group, and that also made him a little nervous. I coaxed him over certain rocks and shifted my weight to indicate to him to go around certain others, but he kept stumbling.

We came to a narrow place in the trail. On one side was a steep shale cliff and on the other, a long drop into a river. Rocky stopped and waited for my direction. We both knew that one wrong move would plummet us into the river below. I guided him toward the gorge, subtly shifting my weight toward the high wall of shale. I thought that if he slipped, I could jump off and save myself.

The moment I shifted, Rocky stopped cold and craned his head around to look at me. He knew exactly what I was doing. I could tell that he was shocked and hurt that I was planning to abandon him. The look in his eye said, "You and me together, right?" Seeing how terrified he was, I shifted my weight back. He swung his head forward in relief, and we negotiated the trail together with no problems.

It's that kind of connection that I think we can all have with our own minds. In *shamatha* meditation . . . we train our minds in stability, clarity, and strength. Through this most basic form of sitting meditation, we discover that we can abide peacefully. . . . It is the first step to becoming a buddha, which literally means "awakened one." We all have the potential to awaken from the sleep of ignorance to the truth of reality.

—Sakyong Mipham, *Turning the Mind into an Ally*

A PEBBLE IN THE RIVER

Mindfulness is the miracle by which we master and restore ourselves. It is the miracle which can call back in a flash our dispersed mind and restore it to wholeness so that we can live each minute of life. Often it helps to meditate on the image of a pebble thrown into a river.

Sit down in whatever position suits you best. Breathe slowly and deeply, following each breath. Then let go of everything. Imagine yourself as a pebble which has been thrown into a river, [falling] effortlessly. . . . the shortest distance possible, finally reaching the bottom, the point of perfect rest. When you feel yourself resting like a pebble which has reached the riverbed, that is the point you begin to find your own rest. If you cannot find joy in peace in these very moments of sitting, then you will be incapable of living in the future when it has become the present.

This spot where you sit is your own spot. It is on this very spot and in this very moment that you can become enlightened.

—Thich Nhat Hanh, adapted from
The Miracle of Mindfulness

THE BODY OF THE BUDDHA

All time is here in this body, which is the body of Buddha. The past exists in its memory and the future in its anticipation, and both of these are now, for when the world is inspected directly and clearly, past and future times are nowhere to be found.

—Alan Watts, *The Way of Zen*

THE MOVIE MAKER

One of the best ways to explain how mindfulness works is through the analogy of the movie theater. When we are watching the screen, we are absorbed in the momentum of the story, our thoughts and emotions manipulated by the images we are seeing. But if just for a moment we were to turn around and look toward the back of the theater at the projector, we would see how these images are being produced. We would recognize that what we are lost in is nothing more than flickering beams of light. Although we might be able to turn back and lose ourselves once again in the movie, its power over us would be diminished. The illusion-maker has been seen.

Similarly, in mindfulness meditations, we look deeply into our own movie-making process. We see the mechanics of how our personal story gets created and how we project that story onto everything we see, hear, taste, smell, think, and do.

Of course, seeing through your own drama sounds terribly unromantic, but that is precisely the point. Mindfulness meditation is meant to be an antidote to sentimentality.

When we see how our personal picture show is created, we no longer have to take the movie quite so personally, and that means a lot less suffering.

Because we are normally lost in the contents of our mind, we also fail to notice what is called in Buddhism "the true nature of mind." We don't recognize the mind's original clarity and openness, or experience the wonder and ease that come from that recognition. Strangely enough, we don't realize this true nature of mind because each of us is standing in the line of sight. With the magic lever of mindfulness we can pull aside the screen of personality and see for ourselves.

To put it another way: when I *see*, I see what I see. What I see when I don't see is "me."

—Wes Nisker, *Buddha's Nature: A Practical Guide to Discovering Your Place in the Cosmos*

WAVES ON A LAKE

Think of your mind as the surface of a lake or of the ocean. There are always waves on the water. Sometimes they are big, sometimes they are small, and sometimes they are almost imperceptible. The water's waves are churned up by winds, which come and go and vary in direction and intensity, just as do the winds of stress and change in our lives, which stir up waves in our minds.

People who don't understand meditation think that it is some kind of special inner manipulation which will magically shut off these waves so that the mind's surface will be flat, peaceful, and tranquil. But just as you can't put a glass plate on the water to calm the waves, so you can't artificially suppress the waves of your mind, and it is not too smart to try. It will only create more tension and inner struggle, not calmness. That doesn't mean that calmness is unattainable. It's just that it cannot be attained by misguided attempts to suppress the mind's natural activity.

It is possible through meditation to find shelter from much of the wind that agitates the mind. Over time, a good deal of the turbulence may die down from lack of continuous feeding. But ultimately the winds of life and of the mind will blow, do what we may. Meditation is about knowing something about this and how to work with it.

—Jon Kabat-Zinn, *Wherever You Go, There You Are: Mindfulness Meditation in Everyday Life*

ONLY THE PRESENT

The measuring of worth and success in terms of time, and the insistent demand for assurances of a promising future, make it impossible to live freely both in the present and in the "promising" future when it arrives. For there is never anything but the present, and if one cannot live there, one cannot live anywhere.

—Alan Watts, *The Way of Zen*

WALDEN POND

Henry David Thoreau's two years at Walden Pond were, above all, a personal experiment in mindfulness. He chose to put his life on the line in order to revel in the wonder and simplicity of present moments. But you don't have to go out of your way or find someplace special to practice mindfulness. It is sufficient to make a little time in your life for stillness and what we call nondoing, and then tune in to your breathing.

All of Walden Pond is within your breath. The miracle of the changing seasons is within the breath; your parents and your children are within the breath; your body and your mind are within the breath. The breath is the current connecting body and mind, connecting us with our parents and our children, connecting our body with the outer world's body. It is the current of life. There are nothing but golden fish in this stream. All we need to see them clearly is the lens of awareness.

—Jon Kabat-Zinn, *Wherever You Go, There You Are:*
Mindfulness Meditation in Everyday Life

A SWINGING DOOR

When we practice zazen our mind always follows our breathing. When we inhale, the air comes into the inner world. When we exhale, the air goes out to the outer world. The inner world is limitless, and the outer world is also limitless. We say "inner world" or "outer world," but actually there is just one whole world. In this limitless world, our throat is like a swinging door. The air comes in and goes out like someone passing through a swinging door. If you think, "I breathe," the "I" is extra. There is no you to say "I." What we call "I" is just a swinging door which moves when we inhale and when we exhale. It just moves; that is all. When your mind is pure and calm enough to follow this movement, there is nothing: no "I," no world, no mind nor body; just a swinging door.

—Shunryu Suzuki, *Zen Mind, Beginner's Mind*

WITHOUT RESISTANCE

Awareness meditation is a way of opening our attention to the truth of what is present. We do not selectively pay attention to pleasant things and ignore the unpleasant. We open choicelessly, to what is positive and joyous as much as to the suffering that we find. Meeting each moment without resistance, we discover unsuspected beauty in our hearts, minds, and bodies, and in the world around us. We sense the uniqueness of each fleeting breath. We perceive the movement of nature within us. We feel sad without needing to justify or eliminate the emotion. We feel happy without needing to believe that we will never again know sadness. This is the way of meditation.

—Gavin Harrison, *In the Lap of the Buddha*

STARK REALITY

Meditation is ruthless in the way it reveals the stark reality of our day-to-day mind. We are constantly murmuring, muttering, scheming, or wondering to ourselves under our breath: comforting ourselves, in a perverse fashion, with our own silent voices. Much of our interior life is characterized by this kind of primary process, almost infantile, way of thinking: "I like this. I don't like that. She hurt me. How can I get that? More of this, no more of that." These emotionally tinged thoughts are our attempts to keep the pleasure principle operative. Much of our inner dialogue, rather than the "rational" secondary process that is usually associated with the thinking mind, is this constant reaction to experience by a selfish, childish protagonist. None of us has moved very far from the seven-year-old who vigilantly watches to see who got more.

Buddhist meditation takes this untrained, everyday mind as its natural starting point, and it requires the development of one particular attentional posture—of naked, or bare, attention. Defined as "the clear and single-minded awareness of what actually happens *to* us and *in* us at the successive moments of perception," bare attention takes this unexamined mind and opens it up, not by trying to change anything but by observing the mind, emotions, and body the way they are. It is the fundamental tenet of Buddhist psychology that this kind of attention is, in itself, healing, that by the constant application of this attentional strategy, all of the Buddha's insights can be realized for oneself. . . . This is what is meant by bare attention: just the *bare* facts and *exact* registering, allowing things to speak for themselves as if seen for the first time, distinguishing any reactions from the core event.

—Mark Epstein, *Thoughts Without a Thinker: Psychotherapy from a Buddhist Perspective*

THE HARMONY OF MINDFULNESS

Mindfulness requires both bare attention to what is and Clear Comprehension of purpose.

Bare Attention heightens the susceptibility and refines the sensitivity of the human mind; Clear Comprehension guides as well as strengthens the actively shaping and creative energies. Bare Attention makes for the growth, preservation, and refinement of intuition—that indispensable source of inspiration and regeneration for the world of action and rational thought. Clear Comprehension, on the other hand, as an active and activating force, works for making the mind a perfect instrument for its hard task of harmonious development and final liberation. It trains one, at the same time, for selfless work in the service of suffering humanity, by bestowing the keen eye of wisdom and the sure hand of skilfulness which are as necessary for that service as a warm heart. Clear Comprehension is capable of giving this training because it provides an excellent schooling in purposeful, circumspect, and selfless action. Hence, Satipatthana [the Path of Mindfulness], in the entirety of both its aspects, produces in the human mind a perfect harmony of *receptivity* and *activity.*

—Nyanaponika Thera, *The Heart of Buddhist Meditation*

WONDER AND LISTEN

The emergence and blossoming of understanding, love, and intelligence has nothing to do with any tradition, no matter how ancient or impressive—it has nothing to do with time. It happens on its own when a human being questions, wonders, inquires, listens, and looks without getting stuck in fear, pleasure, and pain. When self-concern is quiet, in abeyance, heaven and earth are open.

—Toni Packer, *The Work of This Moment*

A MOST ALIVE TASTE

At six P.M., the meditation center served a light meal, usually of fruit and tea. One evening she chose an orange from the big glass bowl, sat down on the grass outside, and prepared to eat. She peeled the orange with the utmost care and tenderness, feeling the juices squirting onto her fingers, noticing with curiosity and pleasure all the white stringy bits. It was as if nothing in the world existed except her and the orange. The smell was so intense, she thought, like the smell of one hundred oranges. She noticed a pleasurable, anticipatory feeling in her mind. When she finally put the orange section in her mouth and bit down onto it, it was the sweetest, most varied, and most alive taste she had ever experienced. She told me it was the first time she had ever really eaten an orange.

In that moment, Stephanie was truly awake.

Being awake is accessible to all of us. It means being fully present to our lives. A meditation retreat, as in Stephanie's case, can bring out this feeling of being alive, but no retreat is necessary in order for us to wake up. Waking up can happen at any moment, in any place, and can be done by anyone. Yet most of us are not awake in our lives; in fact, we have been conditioned to be the opposite, conditioned to space out.

—Diana Winston, *Wide Awake: A Buddhist Guide for Teens*

THE SONG OF THE CHILD

Among one of the tribes of West Africa, when a woman decides that she wishes to have a child, she walks out alone from the village. Perhaps she finds a tree and sits down beneath it. Then she listens. She listens for the song of the child that she has decided to bear. The day she hears that song clearly is considered to be the birthday of the child. She teaches the song to her husband, and it then becomes a part of the mating ritual between the woman and the man. They sing the song during her pregnancy and again when the child is born. It is the song of that child, and it will be sung on each birthday and at each important passage of the child's life. On any wedding day, the song of the groom and the song of the bride are sung together. The last time that song is sung is when that child's body is lowered into its grave.

The path of meditation is like remembering or rediscovering our original song. Through the deepening of self-understanding, we reconnect with ourselves and remember all that has been forgotten. Perhaps we have never known ourselves at all, but if we listen inwardly, we may hear again the beautiful strains of our long-lost melody.

When we hear the song clearly, when we discover our true spirit, we stop blaming or praising others for making us feel bad or good. We no longer feel like victims of circumstance. Rooted in truth, we bend within the winds of circumstance, like fir trees. We engage with the forces in our lives instead of running away from who we are and from all that is painful. In that moment when we are willing to open to the ten thousand joys and the ten thousand sorrows of life, the gateway to our real selves opens. This is the gateway through the palace walls that have kept us isolated and limited for so long. Walking through the gates, we access the possibility of a profound happiness and peace that is not dependent on the conditions of our life.

—Gavin Harrison, *In the Lap of the Buddha*

YOU WILL BE HAPPY

I am quite happy.
If you come to meditate, you will also be happy.

—Dipa Ma in *Knee Deep in Grace:*
*The Extraordinary Life and Teaching of Dipa M*a,
by Amy Schmidt

COMPASSION AND COURAGE

WHAT IS AMAZING

Compassion and love are not mere luxuries. As the source both of inner and external peace, they are fundamental to the continued survival of our species. On the one hand, they constitute nonviolence in action. On the other, they are the source of all spiritual qualities: of forgiveness, tolerance, and all the virtues. Moreover they are the very thing that gives meaning to our activities and makes them constructive. There is nothing amazing about being highly educated; there is nothing amazing about being rich. Only when the individual has a warm heart do these attributes become worthwhile.

—The Dalai Lama,
Ethics for the New Millennium

THE LANGUAGE OF THE HEART

Compassion is not just a feeling; it is a response to pain that is deeply rooted in wisdom. It is a commitment to alleviating suffering and the cause of suffering in all its forms. The human story is both personal and universal. Our personal experiences of pain and joy, grief and despair, may be unique to each of us in the forms they take, yet our capacity to feel grief, fear, loneliness, and rage, as well as delight, intimacy, joy, and ease, are our common bonds as human beings. They are the language of the heart that crosses the borders of "I" and "you." In the midst of despair or pain, you may be convinced that no one has ever felt this way before. Yet there is no pain you can experience that has not been experienced before by another in a different time or place. Our emotional world is universal.

—Christina Feldman, *Compassion: Listening to the Cries of the World*

CHERISH EVERY BEING

[On a summer Dalhousie afternoon, I took tea] with Khamtul Rinpoche, the head of the refugee community from Kham, where with two younger tulkus or incarnate lamas, we were devising plans for their craft production center. As usual, Khamtul Rinpoche had a stretched canvas propped at his side on which, with his customary, affable equanimity, he would be painting as we drank our tea and talked. His huge, round face exuded a serene confidence that our deliberations would bear fruit, just as the Buddha forms on his canvas would take form under the fine, sable brush in his hands.

I, as usual, was seized by more urgency in pushing through plans for the craft cooperative and requests for grants. I could not know that this work would eventuate in the monastic settlement of Tashi Jong, where in a few years, on land acquired up Kangra Valley in the Himalayan foothills, the 400 member community of Khampa monks and laypeople would sink their roots in exile.

On this particular afternoon a fly fell into my tea. This was, of course, a minor occurrence. After a year in India I considered myself to be unperturbed by insects—by ants in the sugar bins, spiders in the cupboard, and even scorpions in my shoes in the morning. Still, as I lifted my cup, I must have registered, by my facial expression or a small grunt, the presence of the fly. Choegyal Rinpoche, the eighteen-year-old tulku who was already becoming my friend for life, leaned forward in sympathy and consternation. "What is the matter?"

"Oh, nothing," I said. "It's nothing, just a fly in my tea." I laughed lightly to convey my acceptance and composure. I did not want him to suppose that mere insects were a problem for me; after all, I was a seasoned India-wallah, relatively free of Western phobias and attachments to modern sanitation.

Choegyal crooned softly, in apparent commiseration with my plight, "Oh, oh, a fly in the tea."

"It's not a problem," I reiterated, smiling at him reassuringly. But he continued to focus great concern on my cup. Rising from his chair, he leaned over and inserted his finger into my tea. With great care he lifted out the offending fly—and then exited from the room. The conversation at the table resumed. I was eager to secure Khamtul Rinpoche's agreement on plans to secure the high-altitude wool he desired for the carpet production.

When Choegyal Rinpoche reentered the cottage, he was beaming. "He is going to be all right," he told me quietly. He explained how he had placed the fly on a leaf of a branch of a bush by the door, where his wings could dry. And the fly was still alive, because he began fanning his wings, and we could confidently expect him to take flight soon. . . .

That is what I remember of that afternoon—not the agreements we reached or plans we devised, but Choegyal's report that the fly would live. And I recall, too, the laughter in my heart. I could not, truth to tell, share Choegyal's dimensions of compassion, but the pleasure in his face revealed how much I was missing by not extending my self-concern to *all* beings, even to flies. Yet this very notion that it was possible gave me boundless delight.

—Joanna Macy, *World as Lover, World as Self*

THE MOON SHINES

In the Buddhist teachings . . . the symbol for compassion is one moon shining in the sky while its image is reflected in one hundred bowls of water. The moon does not demand, "If you open to me, I will do you a favor and shine on you." The moon just shines. The point is not to want to benefit anyone or make them happy. There is no audience involved, no "me" and "them." It is a matter of an open gift, complete generosity without the relative notions of giving and receiving. That is the basic openness of compassion: opening without demand. Simply be what you are, be the master of the situation.

—Chögyam Trungpa, *Cutting Through Spiritual Materialism*

THE UNIVERSAL LANGUAGE

Your emotional world is both personal and universal. As you open to the rhythms of your heart, you meet a lifetime's accumulation of sorrow, grief, and hurt. You encounter your capacity for rage, resentment, harshness, and fear. You also meet your capacity for tenderness, intimacy, and joy. The language of your emotions is universal—grief, sadness, the longing to love and be loved, the capacity to experience and to inflict hurt. The language of your heart teaches you about your interconnectedness and your interdependence. You can reach out to someone who is grieving because you know what grief is. You can comfort someone who is hurt, fearful, or sad because you know the contours of those feelings in your own heart. You can hold another person's sorrow in the tenderness of compassion because you know what it means to be held in the compassion of another.

—Christina Feldman, *Compassion:
Listening to the Cries of the World*

THE AWAKENED HEART

When you awaken your heart . . . you find, to your surprise, that your heart is empty. You find that you are looking into outer space. What are you, who are you, where is your heart? If you really look, you won't find anything tangible and solid. Of course, you might find something very solid if you have a grudge against someone or you have fallen possessively in love. But that is not awakened heart. If you search for awakened heart, if you put your hand through your rib cage and feel for it, there is nothing there except for tenderness. You feel sore and soft, and if you open your eyes to the rest of the world, you feel tremendous sadness. This kind of sadness doesn't come from being mistreated. You don't feel sad because someone has insulted you or because you feel impoverished. Rather, this experience of sadness is unconditioned. It occurs because your heart is completely exposed. There is no skin or tissue covering it; it is pure raw meat. Even if a tiny mosquito lands on it, you feel so touched. Your experience is raw and tender and so personal. It is this tender heart of a warrior that has the power to heal the world.

—Chögyam Trungpa, *Shambhala: The Sacred Path of the Warrior*

ARE YOU BLIND?

Imagine walking along a sidewalk with your arms full of groceries, and someone roughly bumps into you so that you fall and your groceries are strewn over the ground. As you rise up from the puddle of broken eggs and tomato juice, you are ready to shout out, "You idiot! What's wrong with you? Are you blind?" But just before you can catch your breath to speak, you see that the person who bumped into you is actually blind. He, too, is sprawled in the spilled groceries, and your anger vanishes in an instant, to be replaced by sympathetic concern: "Are you hurt? Can I help you up?"

Our situation is like that. When we clearly realize that the source of disharmony and misery in the world is ignorance, we can open the door of wisdom and compassion.

—B. Alan Wallace, *Tibetan Buddhism from the Ground Up:*
A Practical Approach for Modern Life

MACARONI AND CHEESE

A few years ago I was with a close woman friend in a grocery store in California. As we snaked along the aisles, we
become aware of a mother with a small boy moving in the
opposite direction and meeting us head-on in each aisle.
The woman barely noticed us because she was so furious
at her little boy, who seemed intent on pulling items off
the lower shelves. As the mother became more and more
frustrated, she started to yell at the child and several aisles
later had progressed to shaking him by the arm.

At this point my friend spoke up. A wonderful mother
of three and founder of a progressive school, she had
probably never once in her life treated a child so harshly. I
expected my friend would give this woman a solid mother-
to-mother talk about controlling herself and about the
effect this behavior has on a child. Braced for a confronta-
tion, I felt a spike in my already elevated adrenaline.

Instead, my friend said, "What a beautiful little boy. How
old is he?" The woman answered cautiously, "He's three."
My friend went on to comment about how curious he
seemed and how her own three children were just like him

in the grocery store, pulling things off shelves, so interested in all the wonderful colors and packages. "He seems so bright and intelligent," my friend said. The woman had the boy in her arms by now, and a shy smile came upon her face. Gently brushing his hair out of his eyes, she said, "Yes, he's very smart and curious, but sometimes he wears me out." My friend responded sympathetically, "Yes, they can do that; they are so full of energy."

As we walked away, I heard the mother speaking more kindly to the boy about getting home and cooking his dinner. "We'll have your favorite—macaroni and cheese," she told him.

—Catherine Ingram, *Passionate Presence: Seven Qualities of Awakened Awareness*

THE REAL DANGER

An elderly monk found his way to Dharamsala in India after twenty years of imprisonment. Meeting with the Dalai Lama, he told his story, recounting the years of torture, brutality, and isolation. Then the Dalai Lama asked the monk, "Was there any time you felt that your life was truly in danger?" The old monk answered, "The only times I felt deeply endangered were the moments I felt in danger of losing my compassion for my jailers." This is a story of a profound commitment to compassion, a story of faith and forbearance that bears witness to a human being's dedication to keeping his heart and dignity intact in the face of the greatest adversity. The stooped, wrinkled old monk was a simple man without credentials, education, or sophistication. He was also a man with a remarkable heart, who had chosen to forsake the pathways of bitterness and rage, knowing that in following those ways he risked losing what was most precious to him—the home he had made in compassion

—Christina Feldman, *Compassion: Listening to the Cries of the World*

THE ENEMY'S GIFT

Now, as a genuine practitioner of compassion and bodhi-citta, you must develop tolerance. And in order to practice sincerely and to develop patience, you need someone who willfully hurts you. Thus, these people give us real oppor-tunities to practice these things. They are testing our inner strength in a way that even our guru cannot. Even the Buddha possesses no such potential. Therefore, the enemy is *the only one* who gives us this golden opportunity. This is a remarkable conclusion, isn't it! By thinking along these lines and using these reasons, you will eventually develop a kind of extraordinary respect towards your enemies.

—The Dalai Lama, *The World of Tibetan Buddhism: An Overview of Its Philosophy and Practice*

AMITABHA'S VOW

"If, after obtaining Buddhahood, anyone in my land
        gets tossed in jail on a vagrancy rap, may I
        not attain highest perfect enlightenment.

        wild geese in the orchard
        frost on the new grass

"If, after obtaining Buddhahood, anyone in my land
        loses a finger coupling boxcars, may I
        not attain highest perfect enlightenment.

        mare's eye flutters
        jerked by the lead-rope
        stone-bright shoes flick back
        ankles trembling: down steep rock

"If, after obtaining Buddhahood, anyone in my land
        can't get a ride hitch-hiking all directions, may I
        not attain highest perfect enlightenment."

—Gary Snyder, *Myths & Texts*

SITTING WITH THE
DEMONS OF WAR

I had served as a field medical corpsman with the Marine Corps ground forces in the early days of the war in the mountainous provinces on the border of what was then North and South Vietnam. Our casualty rates were high, as were those of the villagers we treated when circumstances permitted.

It had been eight years since my return when I attended my first meditation retreat. At least twice a week for all those years, I had sustained the same recurring nightmares common to many combat veterans: dreaming that I was back there facing the same dangers, witnessing the same incalculable suffering, waking suddenly alert, sweating, scared. At the retreat, the nightmares did not occur during sleep; they filled the mind's eye during the day, at sittings, during walking meditations, at meals. Horrific wartime flashbacks were superimposed over a quiet redwood grove at the retreat center. Sleepy students in the dormitory became body parts strewn about a makeshift morgue on the DMZ. What I gradually came to see was that as I relived these memories as a thirty-year-old spiritual seeker, I was also enduring for the first time the full emotional impact of experiences that, as a twenty-year-old medic, I was simply unprepared to withstand.

I began to realize that my mind was gradually yielding up memories so terrifying, so life-denying, and so spiritually eroding that I had ceased to be consciously aware that I was still carrying them around. I was, in short, beginning to undergo a profound catharsis by openly facing that which I had most feared and therefore most strongly suppressed.

At the retreat I was also plagued by a more current fear: that having released the inner demons of war I would be unable to control them, that they would now rule my days as well as my nights, but what I experienced instead was just the opposite. The visions of slain friends and dismembered children gradually gave way to other half-remembered scenes from that time and place: the entrancing, intense beauty of a jungle forest, a thousand different shades of green, a fragrant breeze blowing over beaches so white and dazzling they seemed carpeted by diamonds.

What also arose at the retreat for the first time was a deep sense of compassion for my past and present self: compassion for the idealistic, young would-be physician forced to witness the unspeakable obscenities of what humankind is capable, and for the haunted veteran who could not let go of memories he could not acknowledge he carried.

Since the first retreat, the compassion has stayed with me. Through practice and continued inner relaxation, it has grown to sometimes encompass those around me as well, when I'm not too self-conscious to let it do so. While the memories have also stayed with me, the nightmares have not. The last of the sweating screams happened in silence, fully awake, somewhere in Northern California many years ago.

—Lloyd Burton in *The Wise Heart: A Guide to the Universal Teachings of Buddhist Psychology*, by Jack Kornfield

STOP THE WAR

We human beings are constantly in combat, at war to escape the fact of being so limited by so many circumstances we cannot control. But instead of escaping, we continue to create more suffering, waging war with good, waging war with evil, waging war with what is small, waging war with what is big, waging war with what is short or long or right or wrong, courageously carrying on the battle.

—Ajahn Chah in *A Still Forest Pool: The Insight Meditation of Achaan Chah*, by Jack Kornfield and Paul Breiter

WHO IS BOTHERING WHOM?

In our practice, we think that noises, cars, voices, sights, are distractions that come and bother us when we want to be quiet. But who is bothering whom? Actually, we are the ones who go and bother them. The car, the sound, is just following its own nature. We bother things through some false idea that they are outside us and cling to the ideal of remaining quiet, undisturbed.

Learn to see that it is not things that bother us, that we go out to bother them. See the world as a mirror. It is all a reflection of mind. When you know this, you can grow in every moment, and every experience reveals truth and brings understanding.

—Ajahn Chah in *A Still Forest Pool: The Insight Meditation of Achaan Chah*, by Jack Kornfield and Paul Breiter

BELOW THE STORM

We should remember that the goal of Buddhist training is not to leave this world for a better world or heaven. We can find peace in this very world, but because our innate peaceful nature is so often obscured, we stagger about like wounded people dealing with the struggles of life. Pure perception can heal us. If we train our minds to accept problems as positive, even very difficult problems can become a source of joy instead of suffering.

Suffering can be a great teacher. Disappointment can wake us up. If life is easy, we may never realize true peace. But if, for example, we lose our money, it can inspire us to find the truth. Maybe we should learn not to care so much about money, and we would know what peace and strength are. Some people who are extremely poor are very cheerful. This shows how relative suffering is, and how the mind can find happiness whatever the external situation.

We should remember that below the storms of our surface worries lies peace. We can heal our suffering by skillfully dealing with life's problems. Everything is impermanent and changing. Instead of seeing change as negative, see it as positive and take advantage of it. That which is impermanent, because of its changing nature, allows us to improve our lives, if we so choose.

Even the most difficult problems, such as serious illness and the decay of the body as it ages, can be viewed positively. We tend to see "self" as permanent, but in fact self, with all its cravings and clingings, is not solid. When pain comes, all our illusions crumble and are swept away like a sand castle being washed out to sea with the first big wave. Family, house, career, all the cherishable things of life, will disappear some day.

But we can see even the most extreme moments, when the body suffers ravaging illness or when death approaches, as joyous and positive opportunities. It is then that we may see the truth about letting go of self.

—Tulku Thondup, *The Healing Power of Mind: Simple Meditation Exercises for Health, Well-Being, and Enlightenment*

PAPER COVERS ROCK

As a child, I loved the game you play by making different shapes with your hands: rock, paper, scissors. I especially loved the moment when "paper" covered "rock." I was enchanted with the idea that something as soft and pliable as paper could conquer something as hard as rock. But then there was always the painful moment when scissors cut into paper. . . . The game could never end, because no one was invulnerable. When I discovered meditation, it was as though I discovered the shape that could rise to meet any obstacle.

—Noelle Oxenhandler, "Where Does It End"

HALLOWEEN GHOSTS

We create big problems for ourselves by not recognizing mind energies when they arrive dressed up in stories. They are like the neighbor's children disguised as Halloween ghosts. When we open the door and find the child next door dressed in a sheet, even though it looks like a ghost, we remember it is simply the child next door. And when I remember the dramas of my life are the energies of the mind dressed in the sheet of a story, I manage them more gracefully.

—Sylvia Boorstein, *It's Easier Than You Think: The Buddhist Way to Happiness*

NO TROUBLE

Sometimes, when someone would come to her with their troubles, she would laugh and laugh. She couldn't stop laughing. Finally, she would say, "This problem you are facing is no problem at all. It is because you think, 'This is mine.' It is because you think, 'There is something for me to solve.' Don't think in this way, and then there will be no trouble."

—Dipa Ma in *Knee Deep in Grace:*
The Extraordinary Life and Teaching of Dipa Ma,
by Amy Schmidt

YOUR MIND

Your mind is all stories.

—Dipa Ma in *Knee Deep in Grace:*
*The Extraordinary Life and Teaching of Dipa M*a,
by Amy Schmidt

THE LION'S ROAR

The "Lion's Roar" is the fearless proclamation that any state of mind, including the emotions, is a workable situation, a reminder in the practice of meditation. We realize that chaotic situations must not be rejected. Nor must we regard them as regressive, as a return to confusion. We must respect whatever happens to our state of mind. Chaos should be regarded as extremely good news.

—Chögyam Trungpa, *The Myth of Freedom and the Way of Meditation*

THE CHARIOT TO DHARMA

We must surrender our hopes and expectations, as well as our fears, and march directly into disappointment, work with disappointment, go into it, and make it our way of life, which is a very hard thing to do. Disappointment is a good sign of basic intelligence. It cannot be compared to anything else: it is so sharp, precise, obvious, and direct. If we can open, then we suddenly begin to see that our expectations are irrelevant compared with the reality of the situations we are facing. This automatically brings a feeling of disappointment.

Disappointment is the best chariot to use on the path of the dharma.

—Chögyam Trungpa, *Cutting Through Spiritual Materialism*

THE MARROW OF MEDITATION

Suppose your children are suffering from a hopeless disease. You do not know what to do; you cannot lie in bed. Normally the most comfortable place for you would be a warm comfortable bed, but now because of your mental agony, you cannot rest. You may walk up and down, in and out, but this does not help. Actually the best way to relieve your mental suffering is to sit in zazen, even in such a confused state of mind and bad posture. If you have no experience of sitting in this kind of difficult situation, you are not a Zen student. No other activity will appease your suffering. In other restless positions, you have no power to accept your difficulties, but in the zazen posture which you have acquired by long, hard practice, your mind and body have great power to accept things as they are, whether they are agreeable or disagreeable.

When you feel disagreeable, it is better for you to sit. There is no other way to accept your problem and work on it. Whether you are the best horse or the worst, or whether your posture is good or bad is out of the question.

Everyone can practice zazen and in this way work on his problems and accept them.

When you are sitting in the middle of your own problem, which is more real to you: your problem or you yourself? The awareness that you are here, right now, is the ultimate fact. This is the point you will realize by zazen practice. In continuous practice, under a succession of agreeable and disagreeable situations, you will realize the marrow of Zen and acquire its true strength.

—Shunryu Suzuki, *Zen Mind, Beginner's Mind*

NOT ONE VIEW

In the understanding of One Dharma, the highest teaching is not one view or another, but what actually works for each of us at any given time. If we understand the various points of view as different skillful means to liberate our minds, then we can actually use each of them to complement each other, rather than seeing them in opposition.

—Joseph Goldstein, *One Dharma:*
The Emerging Western Buddhism

A MARVELOUS BENEFIT

By training the mind and bringing about an inner discipline, you can change your outlook and, thus, your behavior as well. Take my own case, for instance. People usually regard Tibetans who come from Amdo as short-tempered. So in Tibet, when someone would lose his or her temper, people would often take it as a sign that the person was from Amdo! This is the region that I come from. However, if I compare my temperament now to the way it was when I was between the ages of fifteen and twenty, I perceive a noticeable change. These days, I hardly find myself being irritated, and even when I am, it doesn't last long. This is a marvelous benefit—now I am always quite cheerful! It is, I think, the result of my own practice and training. In my lifetime, I have lost my country and have been reduced to being totally dependent on the goodwill of others. I have also lost my mother, and most of my tutors and gurus have passed away, although I now have a few new gurus. Of course, these are tragic incidents, and I feel sad when I think about them. However, I don't feel overwhelmed by sadness. Old, familiar faces disappear, and new faces appear, but I still maintain my happiness and peace of mind. This capacity to relate to events from a broader perspective is, for me, one of the marvels of human nature.

—The Dalai Lama, *The World of Tibetan Buddhism: An Overview of Its Philosophy and Practice*

DON'T HATE YOURSELF

Self-hatred is truly an epidemic in the developed world. U.S. citizens have so much wealth, but they have a poverty of spirit. There is a very revealing story about His Holiness the Dalai Lama, the spiritual leader of Tibet, who was meeting with a group of Buddhist teachers from the United States and Europe. One of the teachers said to him, "A great obstacle to meditation practice of many of my students is extreme self-hatred. What can I do about this?" Apparently the Dalai Lama did not understand what the teacher was asking. He had to have the question translated from English to Tibetan about three or four times. Finally he asked, "Why would anyone want to hate themselves?"

Spiritual practice will help you accept yourself as you are with your own particular quirks; it will also help you see the Buddha nature within you—the unchanging part of you, beyond all quirks.

—Diana Winston, *Wide Awake: A Buddhist Guide for Teens*

WHY CAN'T I?

When I first heard the word *self-hatred* and was first exposed to this concept, I was quite surprised. The reason I found it quite unbelievable is that as practicing Buddhists, we are working very hard to overcome our self-centered attitude and selfish thoughts. So to think of the possibility of someone hating themselves was quite unbelievable. From the Buddhist point of view, self-hatred is very dangerous because even to be in a discouraged state of mind or depressed is seen as a kind of extreme.

The antidote is seen in our natural Buddha-nature, the acceptance or belief that every sentient being, particularly a human being, has Buddha-nature. There is a potential to become a Buddha. Even such weak sentient beings as flies, bees, and insects possess Buddha-nature. Then why not I, who am a human being and possess human intelligence, why can't I also become fully enlightened?

—The Dalai Lama, adapted from *Healing Anger*

NOTICE THE GOOD

Whatever the cause of unworthy feelings, a powerful remedy lies in the realization that we are perfect in our true nature. If we understand this, confidence and fulfillment will spontaneously arise within us. It is crucial to recognize the importance of this understanding, at least on the conceptual level. Then, if we have any positive quality in our lives, however small, we should train ourselves to notice and feel good about it. This is the way to build the habit of a positive mind. When we experience and accept positive energy, even if it grows out of some simple experience, it will bring a feeling of satisfaction that will enable us to develop greater joy and fulfillment.

—Tulku Thondup, *The Healing Power of Mind:*
Simple Meditation Exercises for Health,
Well-Being, and Enlightenment

ENDLESS POSSIBILITIES

If you are on a spiritual path, of course you can be you! Being a spiritual person does not require not having your preferences. You can be a meditator who has a navel ring, or a Buddhist who wears lipstick, or a guy who plays guitar, or who likes punk rock shows....The possibilities are endless.

—Diana Winston, *Wide Awake:*
A Buddhist Guide for Teens

GO FOR BROKE

Once we decide that we really want to go for broke, for perfected truth, once we're being pulled that way in our guts and we finally say, "I don't want anything else, I just want to go," (which is usually a lie, but we're still saying it) that pull, that reaching, draws down upon us all kinds of forces which help that thing happen. That's called grace. There are many beings, both on this plane and on other planes, that are available to guide us and help us, but they don't come unless we want them. Our reaching elicits their help.

—Ram Dass, *Grist for the Mill*

HEAT YOUR POT

Going into retreat gives the opportunity for the [inner] food to cook. . . . You have to put all the ingredients into a pot and stew it up. And you have to have a constant heat. If you keep turning the heat on and off, it is never going to be done. The retreat is like living in a pressure-cooker. Everything gets cooked much quicker. That is why it is recommended.

Even for short periods, it can be helpful. You don't have to do it all your life. I think it would be very helpful for many people to have some period of silence and isolation to look within and find out who they really are when they're not so busy playing roles—being the mother, wife, husband, career person, everybody's best friend, or whatever façade we put up to the world as our identity. It's very good to have an opportunity to be alone with oneself and see who one really is behind all the masks.

— Tenzin Palmo, in *Cave in the Snow:
Tenzin Palmo's Quest for Enlightenment* by Vicki Mackenzie

STAY WITH YOUR BROKEN HEART

When anyone asks me how I got involved in Buddhism, I always say it was because I was so angry with my husband. The truth is that he saved my life. When that marriage fell apart, I tried hard—very, very hard—to go back to some kind of comfort, some kind of security, some kind of familiar resting place. Fortunately for me, I could never pull it off. Instinctively I knew that annihilation of my old dependent, clinging self was the only way to go. . . .

Life is a good teacher and a good friend. Things are always in transition, if we could only realize it. Nothing ever sums itself up in the way that we like to dream about. The off-center, in-between state is an ideal situation, a situation in which we don't get caught and we can open our hearts and minds beyond limit. It's a very tender, non-aggressive, open-ended state of affairs.

To stay with that shakiness—to stay with a broken heart, with a rumbling stomach, with the feeling of hopelessness and wanting to get revenge—that is the path of true awakening. Sticking with that uncertainty, getting the knack of relaxing in the midst of chaos, learning not to panic—this is the spiritual path. Getting the knack of catching ourselves, of gently and compassionately catching ourselves, is the path of the warrior. We catch ourselves one zillion times as once again, whether we like it or not, we harden into resentment, bitterness, righteous indignation—harden in any way, even into a sense of relief, a sense of inspiration.

Every day we could think about the aggression in the world, in New York, Los Angeles, Halifax, Taiwan, Beirut, Kuwait, Somalia, Iraq, everywhere. All over the world, everybody always strikes out at the enemy, and the pain escalates forever. Every day we could reflect on this and ask ourselves, "Am I going to add to the aggression in the world?" Every day, at the moment when things get edgy, we can just ask ourselves, "Am I going to practice peace, or am I going to war?"

—Pema Chödrön, *When Things Fall Apart:*
Heart Advice for Difficult Times

FEED THE DEMONS

Normally we empower our demons by believing that they are real and strong in themselves and have the power to destroy us. As we fight against them, they get stronger. But when we acknowledge them by discovering what they really need, and nurture them, our demons release their hold, and we find that they actually do not have power over us. By nurturing the shadow elements of our being with infinite generosity, we can access the state of luminous awareness and undermine ego. By feeding the demons, we resolve conflict and duality, finding our way to unity.

Demons are ultimately part of the mind and, as such, have no independent existence. Nonetheless, we engage with them as though they were real, and we believe in their existence—ask anyone who has fought post-traumatic stress, or addiction, or anxiety. Demons show up in our lives whether we provoke them or not, whether we want them or not. The mind perceives demons as real, so we get caught up in battling with them. Usually this habit of fighting against our perceived problems gives demons strength rather than weakening them. In the end, all demons are rooted in our tendency to create polarization. By understanding how to work with this tendency to try to dominate the perceived enemy and to see things as either/or, we free ourselves from demons by eliminating their very source.

—Tsultrim Allione, *Feeding Your Demons: Ancient Wisdom for Resolving Inner Conflict*

RISK YOURSELF

The one who, being really on the way, falls upon hard times in the world will not, as a consequence, turn to friends who offer refuge and comfort and encourage the old self to survive. Rather, they will seek out someone who will faithfully and inexorably help them to risk themselves, so that they may endure the suffering and pass courageously through it. . . . Only to the extent that we expose ourselves over and over again to annihilation can that which is indestructible arise within him. In this lies the dignity of daring.

—Karlfried Graf Dürckheim, *The Way of Transformation: Daily Life as Spiritual Practice*

WHEN EVERYTHING IS NOTED

If everything is noted, all your emotional difficulties will disappear. When you feel happy, don't get involved with the happiness. And when you feel sad, don't get involved with it. Whatever comes, don't worry. Just be aware of it.

—Dipa Ma in *Knee Deep in Grace: The Extraordinary Life and Teaching of Dipa Ma*, by Amy Schmidt

SHARP ROCKS ON THE ROAD

In a sense, our path is not a path. The object is not to get somewhere. There is no great mystery, really; what we need to do is straightforward. I don't mean that it is easy; the "path" of practice is not a smooth road. It is littered with sharp rocks that can make us stumble or that can cut right through our shoes. Life itself is hazardous. Encountering the hazards is usually what brings people into Zen centers. The path of life seems to be mostly difficulties, things that give trouble. Yet the longer we practice, the more we begin to understand that those sharp rocks on the road are in fact like precious jewels; they help us to prepare the proper condition for our lives. The rocks are different for each person. One person might desperately need more time alone; another might desperately need more time with other people. The sharp rock might be working with a nasty person or living with somebody who is hard to get along with. The sharp rocks might be your children, your parents, anyone. Not feeling well could be your sharp rock. Losing your job could be it, or getting a new job and being worried about it. There are sharp rocks everywhere. What changes from years of practice is coming to know something you didn't know before: that there are no sharp rocks—the road is covered with diamonds.

—Charlotte Joko Beck, *Nothing Special: Living Zen*

THE GLASS IS BROKEN

On my first day, I was awakened before dawn to accompany the monks on their early morning alms rounds through the countryside. Clad in saffron robes, clutching black begging bowls, they wove single file through the green and brown rice paddies, mist rising, birds singing, as women and children knelt with heads bowed along the paths and held out offerings of sticky rice or fruits. The houses along the way were wooden structures, often perched on stilts, with thatched roofs. Despite the children running back and forth laughing at the odd collection of Westerners trailing the monks, the whole early morning seemed caught in a hush.

After breakfasting on the collected food, we were ushered into an audience with Ajahn Chah. A severe-looking man with a kindly twinkle in his eyes, he sat patiently waiting for us to articulate the question that had brought us to him from such a distance. Finally, we made an attempt: "What are you really talking about? What do you mean by 'eradicating craving'?" Ajahn Chah looked down and smiled faintly. He picked up the glass of drinking water to his left. Holding it up to us, he spoke in the chirpy Lao dialect that was his native tongue: "You see this goblet? For me, this glass is already broken. I enjoy it; I drink out of it. It holds my water admirably, sometimes even reflecting the sun in beautiful patterns. If I should tap it, it has a lovely ring to it. But when I put this glass on a shelf and the wind knocks it over or my elbow brushes it off the table and it falls to the ground and shatters, I say, 'Of course.' But when I understand that this glass is already broken, every moment with it is precious." Ajahn Chah was not just talking about the glass, of course, nor was he speaking merely of the phenomenal world, the forest monastery, the body, or the inevitability of death. He was also speaking to each of us about the self. This self that you take to be so real, he was saying, is already broken.

—Mark Epstein, *Thoughts Without a Thinker:*
Psychotherapy from a Buddhist Perspective

TRANSIENCY

The basic teaching of Buddhism is the teaching of transiency, or change. That everything changes is the basic truth for each existence. No one can deny this truth, and all the teaching of Buddhism is condensed within it. This is the teaching for all of us. Wherever we go, this teaching is true. This teaching is also understood as the teaching of selflessness. Because each existence is in constant change, there is no abiding self. In fact, the self-nature of each existence is nothing but change itself, the self-nature of all existence. There is no special, separate self-nature for each existence. This is also called the teaching of Nirvana. When we realize the everlasting truth of "everything changes" and find our composure in it, we find ourselves in Nirvana.

—Shunryu Suzuki, *Zen Mind, Beginner's Mind*

FEEL THE IMPERMANENCE

Allow your mind to go further into a sense of death arising in each passing moment. Every move you make is an indication of change and impermanence. Each moment you sit in meditation, manifold degeneration, destruction, and change take place. In light of this, any tendency to feel separate from impermanence and change would be absolute ignorance. Remain in meditation with a genuine awareness of constant impermanence and the urgency arising from this.

—Khandro Rinpoche, *This Precious Life: Tibetan Buddhist Teachings on the Path to Enlightenment*

DIE NOW

By taking a few moments to "die on purpose" to the rush of time while you are still living, you free yourself to have time for the present. By "dying" now in this way, you actually become more alive now. This is what stopping can do. There is nothing passive about it. And when you decide to go, it's a different kind of going because you stopped. The stopping actually makes the going more vivid, richer, more textured. It helps keep all the things we worry about and feel inadequate about in perspective. It gives us guidance.

—Jon Kabat-Zinn, *Wherever You Go, There You Are:*
Mindfulness Meditation in Everyday Life

DID I LOVE WELL?

If you have the privilege of being with a person who is conscious at the time of his or her death, you find the questions such a person asks are very simple, "Did I love well?" "Did I live fully?" "Did I learn to let go?"

These simple questions go to the very center of spiritual life. When we consider loving well and living fully, we can see the ways our attachments and fears have limited us, and we can see the many opportunities for our hearts to open. Have we let ourselves love the people around us, our family, our community, the earth upon which we live? And, did we also learn to let go? Did we learn to live through the changes of life with grace, wisdom, and compassion? Have we learned to shift from the clinging mind to the joy of freedom?

—Jack Kornfield, adapted from *A Path with Heart: A Guide through the Perils and Promises of Spiritual Life*

TRADING PLACES

Richard Baker used to say to his Zen students, "If you're with someone who's dying, and you're not willing to trade places with them at that very moment, you're not really practicing."

When Issan Dorsey was dying of AIDS, Baker came to visit him, saying, "I wish I could trade places with you right now." "Don't worry," responded Dorsey. "You'll get your chance."

—Richard Baker and Issan Dorsey,
"Seventeen American Zen Stories," by Sean Murphy

LIVE IT NOW

The only preparation for death, it turns out, is the moment-to-moment life process. When you live in the present now, and then this present, and then *this* present, when the moment of death comes, you are not living in the future or in the past. The freaky thing about death is the anticipatory fear of it. But you can't tell someone else to live in the present moment unless you yourself are.

—Ram Dass, *Grist for the Mill*

REFUGE IN THE DANCE

Meditation offers a full response to the fear of death. When we look closely into our experience, we see that evanescence and dissolution are everywhere. Seeing, feeling, and knowing the movement of each unrepeatable breath, we sense the truth of change. We observe the birth and death of sounds and smells, the arising and passing away of emotions, and the beginning and end of thoughts. We begin to understand that every passage between moments involves the end of something. No phenomenon ever returns in exactly the same form. We begin to deeply know that our own passage out of life must happen just as swiftly and surely someday. When we take refuge in the arising and dissolution of phenomena, on a momentary level, we begin to dance with the truth of our finality instead of struggling with it. We live *with* our mortality, not just in spite of it.

—Gavin Harrison, *In the Lap of the Buddha*

THE TRUSTING SPIRIT

My days are short, and as I grow weaker,
I experience so much gratitude for my meditation
—not only the joy and ease it brought,
but the hard parts,
for every bored and restless sitting
and every fearful fantasy
and every pain and ache I sat through
and every itch I didn't scratch
was training for kindness,
a training for the muscle for bearing witness
for the trusting spirit
that carries me now as I face my death

—Tamara Engle, member of New York
Insight Meditation Society

NO DEATH, NO FEAR

The day my mother died, I wrote in my journal, "A serious misfortune of my life has arrived." I suffered for more than one year after the passing away of my mother. But one night, in the highlands of Vietnam, I was sleeping in the hut of my hermitage. I dreamed of my mother. I saw myself sitting with her, and we were having a wonderful talk. She looked young and beautiful, her hair flowing down. It was so pleasant to sit there and talk to her as if she had never died. When I woke up, it was about two in the morning, and I felt very strongly that I had never lost my mother. The impression that my mother was still with me was very clear. I understood then that the idea of having lost my mother was just an idea. It was obvious in that moment that my mother is always alive in me.

I opened the door and went outside. The entire hillside was bathed in moonlight. It was a hill covered with tea plants, and my hut was set behind the temple halfway up. Walking slowly in the moonlight through the rows of tea plants, I noticed my mother was still with me. She was the moonlight caressing me as she had done so often, very tender, very sweet . . . wonderful! Each time my feet touched the earth, I knew my mother was there with me. I knew this body was not mine alone but a living continuation of my mother and my father and my grandparents and great-grandparents. Of all my ancestors. These feet that I saw as "my" feet were actually "our" feet. Together my mother and I were leaving footprints in the damp soil.

—Thich Nhat Hanh, *No Death, No Fear:*
Comforting Wisdom for Life

NEITHER PESSIMISTIC
NOR OPTIMISTIC

Buddha Dharma *does not* teach that everything is suffering. What Buddhism does say is that life, by its nature, is difficult, flawed, and imperfect. For most of us, this fact of life hardly merits a news flash. Who among us has a perfect life? Of course, we would like it to be delightful and wonderful all the time. But it's not going to happen. That's the nature of life, and that's the First Noble Truth. From a Buddhist point of view, this is not a judgment of life's joys or sorrows; this is a simple, down-to-earth, matter-of-fact description. The fact is that we will all experience ups and downs no matter who we are. That's part of the roller-coaster ride. Buddhism is neither pessimistic nor optimistic; it is realistic.

—Lama Surya Das, *Awakening the Buddha Within: Tibetan Wisdom for the Western World*

DISMANTLE THE TRANCE

The way out of our cage begins with *accepting absolutely everything* about ourselves and our lives, by embracing with wakefulness and care our moment-to-moment experience. By accepting absolutely everything, what I mean is that we are aware of what is happening within our body and mind in any given moment, without trying to control or judge or pull away. I do not mean that we are putting up with harmful behavior—our own or another's. *This is an inner process of accepting our actual, present-moment experience.* It means feeling sorrow and pain without resisting. It means feeling desire or dislike without judging ourselves for the feeling or being driven to act on it.

This is what I call Radical Acceptance. If we are holding back from any part of our experience, if our heart shuts out any part of who we are and what we feel, we are fueling the fears and feelings of separation that sustain the trance of unworthiness. Radical Acceptance directly dismantles the very foundations of this trance.

—Tara Brach, adapted from *Radical Acceptance*

IN THE HARDEST TIMES

The Buddha said that we are never separated from enlightenment. Even at the times we feel most stuck, we are never alienated from the awakened state. This is a revolutionary assertion. Even ordinary people like us with hang-ups and confusion have this mind of enlightenment called bodhichitta. The openness and warmth of bodhichitta is, in fact, our true nature and condition. Even when our neurosis feels far more basic than our wisdom, even when we're feeling most confused and hopeless, bodhichitta—like the open sky—is always here, undiminished by the clouds that temporarily cover it.

Given that we are so familiar with the clouds, of course, we may find the Buddha's teaching hard to believe. Yet the truth is that in the midst of our suffering, in the hardest of times, we can contact this noble heart of bodhichitta. It is always available, in pain as well as in joy.

—Pema Chödrön, *The Places That Scare You:
A Guide to Fearlessness in Difficult Times*

THE SOFT SPOT

To move from aggression to unconditional loving-kindness can seem like a daunting task. But we start with what's familiar. The instruction for cultivating limitless *maitri* is to first find the tenderness that we already have. We touch in with our gratitude or appreciation—our current ability to feel goodwill. In a very nontheoretical way we contact the soft spot of bodhichitta. Whether we find it in the tenderness of feeling love or the vulnerability of feeling lonely is immaterial. If we look for that soft, unguarded place, we can always find it.

For instance, even in the rock-hardness of rage, if we look below the surface of the aggression, we'll generally find fear. There's something beneath the solidity of anger that feels very raw and sore. Underneath the defensiveness is the brokenhearted, unshielded quality of bodhichitta. Rather than feel this tenderness, however, we tend to close down and protect against the discomfort. That we close down is not a problem. In fact, to become aware of when we do so is an important part of the training. The first step in cultivating loving-kindness is to see when we are erecting barriers between ourselves and others. This compassionate recognition is essential. Unless we understand—in a nonjudgmental way—that we are hardening our hearts, there is no possibility of dissolving that armor. Without dissolving the armor, the loving-kindness of bodhichitta is always held back. We are always obstructing our innate capacity to love without an agenda.

—Pema Chödrön, *The Places That Scare You:
A Guide to Fearlessness in Difficult Times*

FAITH BEYOND FEAR

As long as we are alive, we will experience fear. No matter how deep our faith, when our life is threatened, or we think it is, we will feel afraid. But our reaction to fear can change. One time in India, I went to see a well-known Advaita Vedanta teacher, Poonja. While in his presence one day, I had a powerful sense of connection to everyone else in the room, and by inference, to everybody in the city, in the country, and on the planet. When I told him about it, he said, "Now you'll never feel fear again." I thought, *Yeah, right. Unlikely!*

Not even fifteen minutes later, I was back out on the streets of India as cars, trucks, bicycles, carriages, wagons, people, and animals swirled about the roads in no discernible pattern. Right next to me a pack of dogs went at one another, fighting for scraps of food. Life pressed in too far, too fast—I was afraid all right.

On the one hand, I could have been very disappointed— a scant fifteen minutes of freedom! On the other hand, something was different. I was afraid, but it wasn't the same experience of fear as I usually had. I had a deeper knowledge of the vastness of connection in life, within which fear was arising. I realized that Poonja hadn't meant fear wouldn't come up again in my mind but rather that my relationship to it could transform.

As our faith deepens, the "container" in which fear arises gets bigger. Like a teaspoonful of salt placed in a pond full of fresh water rather than in a narrow glass, if our measure of fear is arising in an open, vast space of heart, we will not shut down around it. We may still recognize it as fear, we may still quake inside, but it will not break our spirit.

—Sharon Salzberg, *Faith*

OPEN TO ANY EXPERIENCE

No one likes pain. No one welcomes adversity. No one wants to feel difficult emotions. If we were to announce someday that we are going to sit down and squarely face our suffering and explore everything that is difficult in our lives, our friends might well be aghast. Yet the process of facing our suffering is not necessarily a gloomy one. It can be the first step in learning to relate to our lives with far greater compassion, openness, and kindness than ever before. It is a pragmatic endeavor, too, for if we are honest with ourselves, we will see that we suffer no matter how hard we try not to. Has there ever been a day without its unpleasant moment? Or a lifetime without accident, illness, or loss?

As the heart opens to suffering, compassion flowers and inner conflict begins to diminish. Events may not be as we would have wished them to be, but as we accept them, we see the beauty of nature shining through what before were regarded as the difficulties of our lives.

—Gavin Harrison, adapted from *In the Lap of the Buddha*

SUCH RELIEF

Pain becomes suffering as we harden to it. Softening is such relief, such grace to just sit lovingly with a modicum of discomfort, remembering all those others at this moment with this same pain in this same body of pain and compassion.

Some, such as [one] old monk who thought that people, like a dying horse, should suffer to the end, think suffering is somehow noble, that pain is holy. I have seen all too many Judgment Day–fearing people dying in great pain because of this hopeful, tortured self-negation.

There is nothing holy about pain. We need to stop deifying our suffering.

Pain, though, does have its benefits. As the Dalai Lama has pointed out, if it were not for pain, there would be no compassion. Pain draws compassion like its opposite, stillness, draws wisdom.

—Stephen Levine, *Turning Toward the Mystery:
A Seeker's Journey*

BASIC GOODNESS

Difficult people are . . . the greatest teachers. Aspiring to rejoice in their good fortune is a good opportunity to investigate our reactions and our strategies. How do we react to their good luck, good health, good news? With envy? With anger? With fear? What is our strategy for moving away from what we feel? Revenge, self-denigration? What stories do we tell ourselves? ("She's a snob." "I'm a failure.") These reactions, strategies, and story lines are what cocoons and prison walls are made of.

Then, right on the spot, we can go beneath the words to the nonverbal experience of the emotion. What's happening in our hearts, our shoulders, our gut? Abiding with the physical sensation is radically different from sticking to the story line. It requires appreciation for this very moment. It is a way of relaxing, a way to train in softening rather than hardening. It allows the ground of limitless joy—basic goodness—to shine through.

—Pema Chödrön, *The Places That Scare You:*
A Guide to Fearlessness in Difficult Times

THE MAGIC GETS THROUGH

Once a cook at Gampo Abbey was feeling very unhappy. Like most of us, she kept feeding the gloom with her actions and her thoughts; hour by hour her mood was getting darker. She decided to try to ventilate her escalating emotions by baking chocolate chip cookies. Her plan backfired, however—she burned them all to a crisp. At that point, rather than dump the burned cookies in the garbage, she stuffed them into her pockets and backpack and went out for a walk. She trudged along the dirt road, her head hanging down and her mind burning with resentment. She was saying to herself, "So where's all this beauty and magic I keep hearing about?"

At that moment, she looked up. There walking toward her was a little fox. Her mind stopped and she held her breath and watched. The fox sat down right in front of her, gazing up expectantly. She reached into her pockets and pulled out some cookies. The fox ate them and slowly trotted away. She told this story to all of us at the abbey, saying, "I learned today that life is very precious. Even when we're determined to block the magic, it will get through and wake us up. That little fox taught me that no matter how shut down we get, we can always look outside our cocoon and connect with joy."

—Pema Chödrön, *The Places That Scare You: A Guide to Fearlessness in Difficult Times*

DEEP HAPPINESS

The problem is not materialism as such. Rather it is the underlying assumption that full satisfaction can arise from gratifying the senses alone. Unlike animals, whose quest for happiness is restricted to survival and to the immediate gratification of sensory desires, we human beings have the capacity to experience happiness at a deeper level, which, when achieved, has the capacity to overwhelm contrary experiences.

—The Dalai Lama,
Ethics for the New Millennium

FREEDOM

THE ONE SEAT

As I see it, the mind is like a single point, the center of the universe, and mental states are like visitors who come to stay at this point for short or long periods of time. Get to know these visitors well. Become familiar with the vivid pictures they paint, the alluring stories they tell, to entice you to follow them. But do not give up your seat—it is the only chair around. If you continue to occupy it unceasingly, greeting each guest as it comes, firmly establishing yourself in awareness, transforming your mind into the one who knows, the one who is awake, the visitors will eventually stop coming back. If you give them real attention, how many times can these visitors return? Speak with them here, and you will know every one of them well. Then your mind will at last be at peace.

—Ajahn Chah in *A Still Forest Pool:
The Insight Meditation of Achaan Chah*,
by Jack Kornfield and Paul Breiter

GRASPING AT WATER

If someone who can't swim falls into the ocean, that person will grasp at the water and sink like a rock. A good swimmer who has trained knows how to relax and become one with the vast ocean. Learning how to swim takes practice, and it helps to have some guidance as we begin. It is the same way with training our minds.

—Tulku Thondup, *The Healing Power of Mind:*
Simple Meditation Exercises for Health,
Well-Being, and Enlightenment

MOON OF TRUTH

One of the salient characteristics of water is its conformability: when put into a round vessel it becomes round; when put into a square vessel it becomes square. We have this same adaptability, but as we live bound and fettered through ignorance of our true nature, we have forfeited this freedom. To pursue the metaphor, we can say that the mind of a Buddha is like water that is calm, deep and crystal clear, and upon which "the moon of truth" reflects fully and perfectly. The mind of the ordinary person, on the other hand, is like murky water, constantly being churned by the gales of delusive thought and no longer able to reflect the moon of truth. The moon nonetheless shines steadily upon the waves, but as the waters are roiled, we are unable to see its reflection. Thus we lead lives that are frustrating and meaningless.

How can we fully illumine our life and personality with the moon of truth? We need first to purify this water, to calm the surging waves by halting the winds of discursive thought.

So long as the winds of thought continue to disturb the water of our Self-nature, we cannot distinguish truth from untruth. It is imperative, therefore, that these winds be stilled. Once they abate, the waves subside, the muddiness clears, and we perceive directly that the moon of truth has never ceased shining.

—Philip Kapleau, *The Three Pillars of Zen: Teaching, Practice, and Enlightenment*

INVITATION TO AWARENESS

Mindfulness practice means that we commit fully in each moment to being present. There is no "performance." There is just this moment. We are not trying to improve or to get anywhere else. We are not even running after special insights or visions. Nor are we forcing ourselves to be non-judgmental, calm, or relaxed. And we are certainly not promoting self-consciousness or indulging in self-preoccupation. Rather, we are simply inviting ourselves to interface with this moment in full awareness, with the intention to embody as best we can an orientation of calmness, mindfulness, and equanimity right here and right now.

—Jon Kabat-Zinn, *Wherever You Go, There You Are:*
Mindfulness Meditation in Everyday Life

FREEDOM FROM THE KNOWN

To be free of all authority, of your own and that of another, is to die to everything of yesterday, so that your mind is always fresh, always young, innocent, full of vigor and passion. It is only in that state that one learns and observes. And for this a great deal of awareness is required, actual awareness of what is going on inside yourself without correcting it or telling it what it should or should not be, because the moment you correct it you have established another authority, a censor.

So now we are going to investigate ourselves together—not one person explaining while you read, agreeing or disagreeing with him as you follow the words on the page, but taking a journey together, a journey of discovery into the most secret corners of our minds. And to take such a journey we must travel light; we cannot be burdened with opinions, prejudices, and conclusions. Forget all you know about yourself. We are going to start as if we knew nothing.

—J. Krishnamurti, adapted from *Freedom from the Known*

THE MAIN FEATURE

Many of us are getting to the point in our spiritual journey where we are no longer trying to get high . . . . We are trying to *be*. And being includes everything. We now recognize that if there is anything at all that can bring us down—anything—our house is built upon sand, and there is fear. And where there is fear, we aren't free. Thus we become motivated to confront the places in ourselves which bring us down—not only to confront them, but to create situations in which to bring them forth. . . . That's the mentality that says, "I want to get done; I want to be liberated in this very birth. I've seen how it could be; I'm tired of just seeing previews of coming attractions; I want to become the main feature."

—Ram Dass, *Grist for the Mill*

BRAVERY

The essence of bravery is being without self-deception. However, it's not so easy to take a straight look at what we do. Seeing ourselves clearly is initially uncomfortable and embarrassing. As we train in clarity and steadfastness, we see things we'd prefer to deny—judgmentalness, pettiness, arrogance. These are not sins, but temporary and workable habits of mind. The more we get to know them, the more they lose their power. This is how we come to trust that our basic nature is utterly simple, free of struggle between good and bad.

—Pema Chödrön, *The Places That Scare You:*
A Guide to Fearlessness in Difficult Times

THE GATEWAY

When we come face-to-face with the fear and pain in our psyche, we stand at the gateway to tremendous renewal and freedom. Our deepest nature is awareness, and when we fully inhabit that, we love freely and are whole. . . . When we stop fighting the energy that has been bound in fear, it naturally releases into the boundless sea of awareness. The more we awaken from the grip of fear, the more radiant and free becomes our heart.

—Tara Brach, *Radical Acceptance*

COURAGE

Some years ago, I was facing a situation of immense difficulty in my practice. For weeks, great pain and anguish permeated my experience. At the very lowest time, in a moment of hopeless despair, when any effort at all seemed impossible, the word "courage" suddenly appeared in my mind. It kept repeating, almost like a mantra, and each time the word sounded in my mind, I could literally feel my heart grow stronger. With some magic of its own, it unhooked that last deep place of aversion and fear about what was happening that was keeping me separate from the experience. It brought forth the courage of simply being. What had been intolerable a moment before became completely acceptable. Courage is not about changing anything or grasping for some better state. It's the valor of truly being present.

—Joseph Goldstein, *One Dharma:*
The Emerging Western Buddhism

FEARLESSNESS

Dipa Ma and I were on an airplane coming to the States from India. It was very, very turbulent, and at one point the plane hit an air pocket and dropped. Drinks and other objects flew up to the ceiling as the plane dropped downward before hitting stable air again. I kind of screamed. Dipa Ma was sitting across the aisle from me, and she reached out and took my hand, and she just held it. Then she whispered, "The daughters of the Buddha are fearless."

—Amy Schmidt, *Knee Deep in Grace:*
The Extraordinary Life and Teaching of Dipa Ma

A LARGE, SPACIOUS MEADOW

Even though you try to put people under some control, it is impossible. You cannot do it. The best way to control people is to encourage them to be mischievous. Then they will be in control in its wider sense. To give your sheep or cow a large, spacious meadow is the way to control him. So it is with people: first let them do what they want, and watch them. This is the best policy. To ignore them is not good; that is the worst policy. The second worst is trying to control them. The best one is to watch them, just to watch them, without trying to control them.

—Shunryu Suzuki, *Zen Mind, Beginner's Mind*

WATER ALWAYS HAS WAVES,
OR THE ESSENCE OF MIND

When you are practicing zazen, do not try to stop your thinking. Let it stop by itself. If something comes into your mind, let it come in, and let it go out. It will not stay long. When you try to stop your thinking, it means you are bothered by it. Do not be bothered by anything. It appears as if something comes from outside your mind, but actually it is only the waves of your mind, and if you are not bothered by the waves, gradually they will become calmer and calmer. . . .

It will take quite a long time before you find your calm, serene mind in your practice. Many sensations come, many thoughts or images arise, but they are just waves of your own mind. Nothing comes from outside your mind. Usually we think of our mind as receiving impressions and experiences from outside, but that is not a true understanding of our mind. The true understanding is that the mind includes everything; when you think something comes from outside it means only that something appears in your mind. Nothing outside yourself can cause any trouble. You yourself make the waves in your mind. If you leave your mind as it is, it will become calm. This mind is called big mind.

That everything is included within your mind is the essence of mind. To experience this is to have religious feeling. Even though waves arise, the essence of your mind is pure; it is just like clear water with a few waves. Actually water always has waves. Waves are the practice of the water. To speak of waves apart from water or water apart from waves is a delusion. Water and waves are one. Big mind and small mind are one. When you understand your mind in this way, you have some security in your feeling. As your mind does not expect anything from outside, it is always filled. A mind with waves in it is not a disturbed mind, but actually an amplified one. Whatever you experience is an expression of big mind.

—Shunryu Suzuki, *Zen Mind, Beginner's Mind*

THE RIVER TO THE SEA

In order to meditate properly, it is necessary to have practiced tranquility meditation. This will pacify all disturbing emotions and allow your mind to remain in one-pointedness. When you first start tranquility meditation, the experience is like water rushing from a mountain top: the mind just keeps running, full of many thoughts. Later, at the second stage, the mind is like the same river when it reaches the plains, running slowly and steadily. Later still, in the last stage, the water in the river reaches the sea and dissolves into it. Diligence and devotion will help you calm the mind in this way, and then you will be able to meditate properly.

—Kalu Rinpoche, *The Dharma: That Illuminates All Beings Impartially Like the Light of the Sun and the Moon*

ONLY LET GO

The practice of "letting go" is very effective for minds obsessed by compulsive thinking. You simplify your meditation practice down to just two words—*letting go*—rather than try to develop this practice and then develop that, and achieve this and go into that, and understand this, and read the Suttas, and study the Abhidhamma, and then learn Pali and Sanskrit, and then the Madhyamika and the Prajna Paramita, and then get ordinations in the Hinayana, Mahayana, Vajrayana, and then write books and become a world renowned authority on Buddhism. Instead of becoming the world's expert on Buddhism and being invited to great international Buddhist conferences, just "let go, let go, let go."

I did nothing but this for about two years—every time I tried to understand or figure things out, I'd say, "let go, let go" until the desire would fade out. So I'm making it very simple for you, to save you from getting caught in incredible amounts of suffering. There's nothing more sorrowful than having to attend international Buddhist conferences! Some of you might have the desire to become the Buddha of the age, Maitreya, radiating love throughout the world—but instead, I suggest just being an earthworm, letting go of the desire to radiate love throughout the world. Just be an earthworm who knows only two words—*let go, let go, let go*. You see, ours is the Lesser Vehicle, the Hinayana, so we only have these simple, poverty-stricken practices!

—Ajahn Sumedho, *Cittaviveka Teachings from the Silent Mind*

FAITH IS IN THE WAITING

I know that sometimes things are so bad that no matter what practices we do or what medications we take, we can't seem to generate even that small amount of faith we need for inspiration to keep going. Then, if we can stand inside our pain awhile and wait, over time we may come to also see it as a way into the deepest parts of ourselves and then back out into the world, a vehicle for new insight into who we are and how much we need to care for ourselves and one another. If there is nothing we can do right now but wait, then, as T. S. Eliot wrote, "the faith is in the waiting." If we can but wait, we may yet emerge from despair with the same understanding that Zen master Suzuki Roshi expressed: "Sometimes, just to be alive is enough."

—Sharon Salzberg, *Faith*

A VAST FABRIC

Experiencing the power of faith doesn't mean we've annihilated fear or denied it or overcome it through strenuous effort. It means that when we think we've conquered fear only to be once again overcome by it, we can still go on. It means feeling our fear and still remaining in touch with our heart, so that fear does not define our entire world.

As we open to what is actually happening in any given moment, we become increasingly aware of our lives as one small part of a vast fabric made of an evanescent, fleeting, shimmering pattern of turnings. Letting go of the futile battle to control, we can find ourselves rewoven into the pattern of wholeness, into the immensity of life, always happening.

We can step out of the hope/fear gyration and give our capacity to love a chance to flower. This is where we can place our faith. Even as we fall, fall endlessly, with faith we are held as we open to each moment.

—Sharon Salzberg, adapted from *Faith*

DON'T LIMIT YOURSELF

In the Tibetan map of the world, the world is a circle, and
at the center there is an enormous mountain guarded by
four gates. And when they draw a map of the world, they
draw the map in sand, and it takes months and then when
the map is finished, they erase it throw the sand into the
nearest river.

Last fall the Dalai Lama came to New York City to do
a two-week ceremony called the Kalachakra which is a
prayer to heal the earth. And woven into these prayers
were a series of vows that he asked us to take and before I
knew it I had taken a vow to be kind for the rest of my life.
And I walked out of there and I thought: "For the rest of
my life?? What have I done? This is a disaster!"

And I was really worried. Had I promised too much?
Not enough? I was really in a panic. They had come from
Tibet for the ceremony and they were walking around
midtown in their new brown shoes and I went up to one
of the monks and said, "Can you come with me to have a
cappuccino right now and talk?" And so we went to this
little Italian place. He had never had coffee before so he

kept talking faster and faster and I kept saying, "Look, I don't know whether I promised too much or too little. Can you help me please?"

And he was really being practical. He said, "Look, don't limit yourself. Don't be so strict! Open it up!" He said, "The mind is a wild white horse and when you make a corral for it make sure it's not too small. And another thing: when your house burns down, just walk away. And another thing: keep your eyes open.

"And one more thing: Keep moving. Cause it's a long way home."

—Laurie Anderson, "Wild White Horses,"
in *What Book!? Buddha Poems from Beat to Hiphop*,
edited by Gary Gach

QUITE SUFFICIENT

As strange as it sounds, meditation may reveal that we are happier than we thought we were. We may discover that ancient conditioning rather than present circumstances is causing our dissatisfaction, and that this moment is quite sufficient or even wonderful, and we simply hadn't noticed.

—Wes Nisker, *Buddha's Nature: A Practical Guide to Discovering Your Place in the Cosmos*

DON'T EXHAUST YOURSELF

Only our searching for happiness
prevents us from seeing it.
It's like a vivid rainbow which you pursue without
ever catching,
or a dog chasing its own tail.
Although peace and happiness do not exist
as an actual thing or place,
it is always available
and accompanies you every instant.

Wanting to grasp the ungraspable,
you exhaust yourself in vain.
As soon as you open and relax this tight fist
of grasping,
infinite space is there—open, inviting, and
comfortable.

Make use of this spaciousness, this freedom
and natural ease.
Don't search any further.

Don't go into the tangled jungle
looking for the great awakened elephant
who is already resting quietly at home
in front of your own hearth.

—Lama Gendun, "Free and Easy"

HOW SIDDHARTHA LISTENED

Siddhartha listened. He was now listening intently, completely absorbed, quite empty, taking in everything. He felt that he had now completely learned the art of listening. He had often heard all this before, all these numerous voices in the river, but today they sounded different. He could no longer distinguish the different voices—the merry voice from the weeping voice, the childish voice from the manly voice. They all belonged to each other: the lament of those who yearn, the laughter of the wise, the cry of indignation, and the groan of the dying. They were all interwoven and interlocked, entwined in a thousand ways. And all the voices, all the goals, all the yearnings, all the sorrows, all the pleasures, all the good and evil, all of them together was the world. All of them together [were] the streams of events, the music of life. When Siddhartha listened attentively to this river, to this song of a thousand voices, when he did not listen only to the sorrow or laughter, did not bind his soul to any one particular voice and absorb it in himself, but heard them all, the whole, the unity—then the great song of a thousand voices consisted of one word: OM—*perfection*.

—Hermann Hesse, *Siddhartha*

ESSENTIAL EMPTINESS

Although the concept that mind is empty of any limiting characteristic may be at least superficially understandable, many people find great difficulty in the idea that what we experience is likewise empty. What does it mean to say that the phenomenal world—this animate and inanimate universe we perceive—is empty? How is that true for this world full of rocks and trees and houses, earth, water, and all the elements, living creatures moving about living their lives?

There is actually no contradiction in saying that something that appears to be so real is essentially empty. We can illustrate this by an example, the dream state.

When we go to sleep at night, we dream. The mind is active in the dream, there is perception of form that is seen, sound that is heard, odors that are smelled, tastes that are tasted, textures that are felt, thoughts that arise. All these happen in the dream state, but when we wake, it is obvious that nothing real was experienced. What occurred had a conventional reality during the dream, but no one will maintain that what took place in the dream happened in the same way things happen in our waking state. The dream was a series of mental projections: it had a conventional, temporary reality, but not an ultimate one. Because the dream lacks an enduring self-nature, we can say that it is empty.

We can think of our perception of the waking world in just such a way. All sorts of ideas, emotions, concepts, and reactions arise in us. Things we experience can make us happy, sad, or angry, can increase our attachment or aversion. But even though all these thoughts and responses arise, none has any nature of its own: we should not take them to be real—they are simply ongoing mental projections produced by particular circumstances. For this reason we can again say that our experience is empty, because it lacks any ultimate self-nature. We can say that no aspect of our experience, of the outer phenomenal world or the inner mental world, has one atom of reality. Nothing we experience is anything more than the mind's perception of its own projections, the reality of which is only conventional.

—Kalu Rinpoche, *The Dharma: That Illuminates All Beings Impartially Like the Light of the Sun and the Moon*

SEE THE ORIGINAL MIND

About this mind—in truth there is nothing really wrong with it. It is intrinsically pure. Within itself it's already peaceful. If the mind is not peaceful these days, it's because it follows moods. The real mind doesn't have anything to it; it is simply an aspect of nature. It becomes peaceful or agitated because moods deceive it. The untrained mind is stupid. Sense impressions come and trick it into happiness, suffering, gladness, and sorrow, but the mind's true nature is none of those things. That gladness or sadness is not the mind, but only a mood coming to deceive us. The untrained mind gets lost and follows these things; it forgets itself. Then we think that it is we who are upset or at ease or whatever.

But really this mind of ours is already unmoving and peaceful—really peaceful! Just like a leaf which remains still so long as the wind doesn't blow. If a wind comes up, the leaf flutters. The fluttering is due to the wind—the fluttering of the mind is due to those sense impressions; the mind follows them. If it doesn't follow them, it doesn't flutter. If we know fully the true nature of sense impressions, we will be unmoved.

Our practice is simply to see the "Original Mind." We must train the mind to know those sense impressions and not get lost in them, to make it peaceful. Just this is the aim of all this difficult practice we put ourselves through.

—Ajahn Chah, *Food for the Heart:*
The Collected Teachings of Ajahn Chah

MIND

Mind creates both
samsara and nirvana.
Yet there is nothing much to it.
It is just thoughts.
Once we recognize that thoughts are empty,
the mind will no longer have the power to deceive us.

—Dilgo Khyentse, "Three Short Teachings"

REALITY BEYOND CONCEPT

On some clear night, go outside, look up at the sky, and see if you can find the Big Dipper. For most people that is a familiar constellation, easy to pick out from all the other stars. But is there really a Big Dipper up there in the sky?

There is no Big Dipper up there. "Big Dipper" is a concept. Humans looked, saw a certain pattern, and then created a concept in our collective mind to describe it. That concept is useful because it helps us recognize the constellation. But it also has another, less useful effect. By creating the concept "Big Dipper," we separate out those stars from all the rest, and then, if we become attached to the idea of that separation, we lose the sense of the night sky's wholeness, its oneness. Does the separation actually exist in the sky? No. We created it through the use of a concept.

Does anything change in the sky when we understand that there in no Big Dipper? No. The stars in the sky remain just the same, and the pattern of the stars remains the same. We simply see that the concept that names the pattern of stars, and that separates those particular ones from all the others, does not have any independent existence.

Likewise, realizing that "self" is a concept revolutionizes our understanding by revealing how things have always been. Each of one us is a constellation of mental-physical processes. We recognize the familiar pattern, name it, and then become so identified with the concept that we fall into the great illusion of believing that some being is ultimately there. "Joseph" is just the same as "Big Dipper." "Joseph" is a concept, a name given to a pattern of stars.

Our practice is to awaken from the illusion of taking concepts to be the reality, so that we can live in a clear awareness of how things actually are. It should be easy to free oneself from attachment to concepts, . . . but it is not. On some clear and starry night, quietly look up at the sky and observe whether it is possible *not* to see the Big Dipper. We have a hard time not seeing it because of strong, conditioned habits of recognition.

In just the same way, by not examining carefully the composite nature of what we call "self," we become attached to the concept and believe it has some inherent existence. We fail to see that what we are is a constellation of rapidly changing elements. Life is a process of becoming, of conditions arising and passing; it is not happening *to* anyone. There is no being behind it to whom it happens.

Meditation helps us see with bare attention just what is

there. We may still use concepts when appropriate, but we do not lose touch with the reality behind them. We learn to look at the sky with a clear and silent mind; we learn to look at ourself with the same clarity and stillness.

—Joseph Goldstein, *Insight Meditation:*
The Practice of Freedom

OBSCURATION
AND ENLIGHTENMENT

Until all [the] levels of confusion and obscuration are elim-
inated, Enlightenment cannot arise. We must recover the
original purity and transparency of water now polluted by
sediment; we must disperse the clouds veiling the sun, so
we can see clearly and receive its warmth directly. Once we
understand through meditation the Emptiness of mind,
its Clarity and Unimpededness, the intense constriction
produced by clinging to self and phenomena begins to
diminish.

—Kalu Rinpoche, *The Dharma: That Illuminates All Beings
Impartially Like the Light of the Sun and the Moon*

THE GATELESS GATE

Today someone asked me if it was possible to reach enlightenment through contemplating emptiness. My answer was no, contemplating emptiness cannot lead you to enlightenment. In fact, no-method can lead you to enlightenment. By using a practice method, you can settle the mind and be at ease without afflictions. Any method can settle the mind in the present moment, but with Silent Illumination, you can be relieved of even the present moment. Just take this attitude: don't worry about the past or the future, and let go of the present too. Just stay in awareness. Chan is called the "gateless gate" because it has no door to enlightenment. The methods fool you into thinking, "Aha, there's a door. Let's find the key." People will look for the key, the right method that will get them enlightened. They search for the door to enlightenment, and not finding it, they may give up. In fact, there is no door. But according to each person's practice and karmic disposition or virtuous roots, suddenly he or she may gain entry and become enlightened. In the process of searching, you finally walk through the gateless gate.

You will suddenly recognize that your nostrils point downward. In other words, you will learn that the possibility of enlightenment was there all along.

—Sheng Yen, *The Method of No-Method:*
The Chan Practice of Silent Illumination

HAPPILY WE LET IT GO

The Buddha said, "I teach only two things—suffering and the end of suffering."

What is the cause of suffering? Suffering arises from clinging. If the mind says, "I am," then there is suffering. If the mind says, "I am not," then there is also suffering. As long as the mind clings, it suffers. When the mind is silent, it becomes peaceful and free.

Clinging has 108 names. It may be called greed, anger, envy, or covetousness. Clinging is like a snake that sheds its skin. Beneath one tough skin, there is always another.

How can we be freed from suffering? We simply let it go. "Painfully we sustain it, happily we let it go." Suffering follows one with an untamed mind as surely as a cart follows an ox. Peacefulness follows one who has mastered the mind as surely as his own shadow.

Clinging always brings suffering. This is the natural law, like the law of fire. It does not matter whether you believe that fire is hot. When you hold fire, it will burn you.

The Dharma teaches us to know, shape, and free the mind. When the mind is mastered, all of the Dharma is mastered. What is the key for mastering the mind? It is mindfulness. Does it take long to be released from suffering? No. Enlightenment is always here and now.

—Maha Ghosananda, *Step by Step: Meditations on Wisdom and Compassion*

YOU ARE EMPTINESS

The purpose of meditation is to find the meditator. When you look for the meditator, you won't find him, her, or it. All you'll find is silent Emptiness. In finding Emptiness, the mind stops. If you let it, Emptiness will stop the mind—unless you run back into samsara, into the mind's drama of thinking, striving, and confusion. When you allow Emptiness to stop your mind, you'll awaken and realize that you are that Emptiness. You'll realize that you are not the mind or the body or any meditative phenomena. You are Emptiness. Emptiness means limitless, boundless, Pure Consciousness.

—Adyashanti, *The Impact of Awakening: Excerpts from the Teachings of Adyashanti*

A STILL MIND

The only silence we know is the silence when noise stops, the silence when thought stops—but that is not silence. Silence is something entirely different, like beauty, like love. And this silence is not the product of a quiet mind, it is not the product of the brain cells which have understood the whole structure and say, "For God's sake, be quiet"; then the brain cells themselves produce the silence and that is not silence. Nor is silence the outcome of attention in which the observer is the observed; then there is no friction, but that is not silence.

You are waiting for me to describe what this silence is so that you can compare it, interpret it, carry it away and bury it. It cannot be described. What can be described is the known, and the freedom from the known can come into being only when there is a dying every day to the known, to the hurts, the flatteries, to all the images you have made, to all your experiences—dying every day so that the brain cells themselves become fresh, young, innocent. But the innocence, that freshness, that quality of tenderness and gentleness, does not produce love: it is not the quality of beauty or silence.

The silence which is not the silence of the ending of noise is only a small beginning. It is like going through a small hole to an enormous, wide, expansive ocean, to an immeasurable, timeless state. But this you cannot understand verbally unless you have understood the whole structure of consciousness and the meaning of pleasure, sorrow, and despair, and the brain cells themselves have become quiet. Then perhaps you may come upon that mystery which nobody can reveal to you and nothing can destroy. A living mind is a still mind, a living mind is a mind that has no center and therefore no space and time. Such a mind is limitless and that is the only truth, that is the only reality.

—J. Krishnamurti, *Freedom from the Known*

OPEN YOUR EYES

This is really the crux of the matter: the contemplative hermit, far from closing his eyes and being dead to the world, opens them and becomes awake; far from blunting his senses, he develops a higher awareness and a deeper insight into the real nature of the world and of his own mind. And this shows him that it is as foolish to run away from the world as to run after the world: both extremes having their root in the illusion that the "world" is something separate from ourselves.

—Lama Anagarika Govinda, *The Way of the White Clouds*

THE EYES OF A BODHISATTVA

If you are a poet, you will see clearly that there is a cloud floating in this sheet of paper. Without a cloud, there will be no water; without water, the trees cannot grow; and without trees, you cannot make paper. So the cloud is in here. The existence of this page is dependent on the existence of a cloud. Paper and cloud are so close. Let us think of other things, like sunshine. Sunshine is very important because the forest cannot grow without sunshine, and we as humans cannot grow without sunshine. So the logger needs sunshine in order to cut the tree, and the tree needs sunshine in order to be a tree. Therefore, you can see sunshine in this sheet of paper. And if you look more deeply, with the eyes of a bodhisattva, with the eyes of those who are awake, you see not only the cloud and sunshine in it, but that everything is here, the wheat that became the bread for the logger to eat, the logger's father—everything is in this sheet of paper. . . .

[This paper is] empty of an independent self. Empty, in this sense, means that the paper is full of everything, the entire cosmos. The presence of this tiny sheet of paper proves the presence of the whole cosmos.

—Thich Nhat Hanh, *Being Peace*

THE DIVINE ABODES

In traditional Buddhist texts, lovingkindness, compassion, sympathetic joy, and equanimity are called the "divine abodes" of the mind. The essence of mind, unencumbered by confusion, is ultimately spacious. It is inherently equanimous, encompassing all things and holding them in an ease-filled balance.

It is from this place of equanimity that spontaneous movements of the mind arise in response to different events. Lovingkindness arises as the spontaneous response to all beings, and compassion arises as a response to pain. Sympathetic joy arises in the shared delight of other people's good fortune when we become aware of it. All three of these movements of heart and mind (of lovingkindness, of compassion, and of sympathetic joy) are the varied reflections of fundamental equanimity.

Equanimity is not empty; equanimity is full of everything.

—Sylvia Boorstein, *It's Easier Than You Think:*
The Buddhist Way to Happiness

THE FEMININE DHARMA

To me, the special female quality (which of course many men have as well) is first of all a sharpness, a clarity. It cuts through—especially intellectual ossification. It's very sharp and gets to the point. [This] principle stands for the intuitive force. Women get it in a flash—they're not interested in intellectual discussion which they normally find dry and cold with minimum appeal. To women, that's the long way of going about it. They go through the back door! This reveals itself as women being more practical in their approach, less . . . entranced by theories and ideas—they want to be able to crunch it between their teeth. . . . Of course, Prajnaparamita is female . . . [referring to the Mother of all Buddhas]. She's the Perfection of Wisdom which cuts away all our concepts and desires to make something very stable and settled. We build up our ideas. We try to make them concrete. She cuts away, cutting, cutting, cutting. She cuts things back to the bare essentials.

At the same time, women have a nurturing, a softness, a gentleness. Women tend to be more into feeling than men, which makes it easier to develop Bodhicitta. Loving kindness is innate in women, because of the mothering factor. A mother is prepared to die for her child. That impulse can be developed towards all beings. Again, it's a matter of feeling, not intellect. These are not just useful qualities—they're essential.

Female spiritual energy is also very quick. Like Tara. You don't have to be a great yogi to communicate with Tara. She's there! Like a mother, she has to be very quick because she can't wait until her child has reached a certain level before she gives it her attention and compassion. She has to be right there with it—from the moment it's born— a little wriggling worm. Whether it's a good child or a bad child, she's there to help.

—Tenzin Palmo in *Cave in the Snow: Tenzin Palmo's Quest for Enlightenment* by Vicki Mackenzie

THE INSPIRATION OF WOMEN

We must still struggle to find spiritual ways that are adapted to us as women and which validate and develop us as women, not as asexual entities who must deny their inherent nature in order to be acceptable on the spiritual path. When we do this, we will certainly be of greater benefit to others than if we are trying to ape men, following traditions that were created by men for men.

Even though I believe that on the absolute level the true nature of the mind has no sexual characteristics, on the relative level the means to achieving illumination must be adapted to the individual. The differences between individuals must be appreciated and even celebrated. Women and men are different when we speak from a relative point of view, but how these differences are interpreted and whether these differences are seen positively or negatively is a matter of cultural and religious conditioning.

In order for women to find viable paths to liberation, we need the inspiration of other women who have succeeded in remaining true to their own energies without becoming fixated on their gender and have, with this integrity, reached complete liberation.

—Tsultrim Allione, *Women of Wisdom*

THE BUDDHA AND THE GODDESS

Thus have I [envisioned]:
    Once the Buddha was walking
    along the forest path in the Oak Grove at Ojai,
    walking without arriving anywhere or having any
    thought of arriving or not arriving.
And lotuses, shining with the morning dew
    miraculously appeared under every step
    Soft as silk beneath the toes of the Buddha.
When suddenly, out of the turquoise sky,
    dancing in front of his half-shut inward-looking
    eyes, shimmering like a rainbow
    or a spider's web
    transparent as the dew on a lotus flower
    —the Goddess appeared quivering
    like a hummingbird in the air before him.
She, for she was surely a she
    as the Buddha could clearly see
    with his eye of discriminating awareness wisdom,

was mostly red in color
though when the light shifted
she flashed like a rainbow.
She was naked except
for the usual flower ornaments
goddesses wear.
Her long hair
was deep blue, her eyes fathomless pits
of space, and her third eye a bloodshot
song of fire.
The Buddha folded his hands together
and greeted the Goddess thus:
"O goddess, why are you blocking my path?
Before I saw you I was happily going nowhere.
Now I'm not so sure where I go."
"You can go around me,"
said the Goddess, twirling on her heel like a bird
darting away,
but just a little way away,
"or you can come after me
but you can't pretend I'm not here,
This is my forest, too."
With that the Buddha sat
supple as a snake
solid as a rock
beneath a Bo tree

        that sprang full-leaved
        to shade him.
"Perhaps we should have a chat,"
        he said.
        "After years of arduous practice
        at the time of the morning star
        I penetrated reality and . . ."
"Not so fast, Buddha," the Goddess said,
        "I am reality."

        The earth stood still,
        the oceans paused,
        the wind itself listened
        —a thousand arhats, bodhisattvas and dakinis
        magically appeared to hear
        what would happen in the conversation.
"I know I take my life in my hands,"
        said the Buddha,
        "But I am known as the Fearless One
        —so here goes."
And he and the Goddess
        without further words
        exchanged glances.
Light rays like sunbeams
        shot forth
        so brightly that even

Sariputra, the All-Seeing One,
    had to turn away.
And then they exchanged thoughts
And the illumination was as bright as a diamond candle
And then they exchanged minds
And there was a great silence as vast as the universe that
    contains everything
And then they exchanged bodies
And then clothes
And the Buddha arose
    as the Goddess
    and the Goddess arose as the Buddha.
And so on back and forth
    for a hundred thousand hundred thousand kalpas.
If you meet the Buddha
    you meet the Goddess.
    If you meet the Goddess,
    you meet the Buddha.
Not only that. This:
    The Buddha is emptiness,
    The Goddess is bliss.
    The Goddess is emptiness,
    The Buddha is bliss.
    And that is what
    And what-not you are
    It's true.

So here comes the mantra of the Goddess and the Buddha, the unsurpassed nondual mantra. Just to say this mantra, just to hear this mantra once, just to hear one word of this mantra once makes everything the way it truly is: OK. So here it is:

Earth-walker / sky-walker
Hey silent one, Hey great talker
Not two / not one
Not separate / not apart
This is the heart
Bliss is emptiness
Emptiness is bliss
Be your breath, Ah
Smile, Hey, And relax, Ho
Remember: You can't miss.

—Rick Fields, "The Buddha and the Goddess," in
Dharma Gaia: A Harvest of Essays in Buddhism & Ecology,
edited by Allan Hunt Badiner

NO RUNNING AWAY

Have you ever noticed that there is no running away from anything? That, sooner or later, the things that you don't want to deal with and try to escape from, or paper over and pretend aren't there, catch up with you—especially if they have to do with old patterns and fears? The romantic notion is that if it's no good over here, you have only to go over there and things will be different. If this job is no good, change jobs. If this wife is no good, change wives. If this town is no good, change towns. If these children are a problem, leave them for other people to look after. The underlying thinking is that the reason for your troubles is outside of you—in the location, in others, in the circumstances. Change the location, change the circumstances, and everything will fall into place; you can start over, have a new beginning.

The trouble with this way of seeing is that it conveniently ignores the fact that you carry your head and your heart, and what some would call your "karma," around with you. You cannot escape yourself, try as you might. And what reason, other than pure wishful thinking, would you have to suspect that things would be different or better somewhere else anyway? Sooner or later, the same problems would arise if in fact they stem in large part from your patterns of seeing, thinking, and behaving. Too often, our lives cease working because we cease working at life, because we are unwilling to take responsibility for things as they are and to work with our difficulties. We don't understand that it is actually possible to attain clarity, understanding, and transformation right in the middle of what is here and now, however problematic it may be.

—Jon Kabat-Zinn, *Wherever You Go, There You Are: Mindfulness Meditation in Everyday Life*

FIDELITY

While unconditional love can be nonattached, there is no such thing as unconditional *relationship*. When our love becomes sexual and thus relational, we impose certain conditions that are nonnegotiable. Fidelity, for example, and kindness and caring actions—if these conditions aren't present, the relationship will be a source of more pain than pleasure and will surely end in a broken heart, fractured spirit, and fatigued mind. Of course, the conditions of relationship don't necessarily have to affect unconditional love, but most often when the container of loving sexual relationship is broken, the love itself is also somehow altered.

When sexuality is related to skillfully, it becomes our teacher rather than our tormentor. It becomes just another experience in the mind and body that we can and should pay close attention to.

—Noah Levine, *Against the Stream:*
A Buddhist Manual for Spiritual Revolutionaries

KARMA

Karma is a Sanskrit word (*kamma* in Pali) that means "action." The law of karma refers to the law of cause and effect: that every volitional act brings about a certain result. If we act motivated by greed, hatred, or delusion, we are planting the seed of suffering; when our acts are motivated by generosity, love, or wisdom, then we are creating the karmic conditions for abundance and happiness. An analogy from the physical world illustrates this: if we plant an apple seed, the tree that grows will bear apples, not mangoes. And once the apple seed is planted, no amount of manipulation or beseeching or complaining will induce the tree to yield a mango. The only meaningful action that will produce a mango is to plant a mango seed. Karma is just such a law of nature, the law of cause and effect on the psychophysical plane.

In Buddhist teaching, *karma* specifically refers to volition, the intention or motive behind an action. He said that karma is volition, because it is the motivation behind the action that determines the karmic fruit. Inherent in each intention in the mind is an energy powerful enough to bring about subsequent results. When we understand that karma is based on volition, we can see the enormous responsibility we have to become conscious of the intentions that precede our actions. If we are unaware of the motives of our minds, when unskillful volitions arise, we may unmindfully act on them and thus create the conditions for future suffering.

The law of karma can be understood on two levels, which indicate the vast scope of its implications in our lives. On one level, *karma* refers to the experience of cause and effect over a period of time. We perform an action, and sometime later, we being to experience its results. We plant a mango seed, and many years later we taste the fruit. The other level of understanding karma has to do with the quality of mind in the very moment of action. When we experience a mind state of love, there naturally comes along with it a feeling of openness and joy that is its immediate fruit; similarly, when there are moments of greed or hatred, in addition to whatever future results will come, we also experience the painful energies that arise with those states. Our direct awareness of how the karmic law is working in each moment can be a strong motivation to develop skillful states of mind that create happiness for us in the moment, as well as produce the fruit of well-being in the future.

When we understand [karma], and live our understanding, when we act on what we know, then we experience a sense of wholeness and peace. If we live in a way that is out of harmony, ignoring the nature of things, we then experience dissonance, pain, and confusion.

—Joseph Goldstein in *Seeking the Heart of Wisdom: The Path of Insight Meditation,* by Joseph Goldstein and Jack Kornfield

KARMA HAS ONE TASTE

If it is the case that all experience is only the projection of mind, what determines the way in which our perceptions take place? The force that influences the way in which mind experiences the world is karma, actions and their results.

On the basis of fundamental ignorance about the real nature of mind, karmic tendencies and other obscurations develop. The fundamental state of unawareness is like the earth, in which seeds can be planted. The seeds represent karmic predispositions, which are reinforced by physical, mental, and verbal actions. Once a seed is planted, it needs support from the earth, and nourishment, water, light, heat: without these, it remains inert. When all the requisite circumstances are present, the seed germinates, grows, flowers, and multiplies. In the same way, the tendency established and reinforced by an action is stored in the fundamental state of confusion and remains latent until circumstances in the environment or in the mind itself provide a channel by which the tendency emerges and comes to fruition as an active part of our existence.

As human beings, we exist in a relatively superior state. This is a result of positive karmic tendencies reinforced by virtuous actions—mental, verbal, and physical—in countless previous lifetimes. All human karma is similar enough for all of us to experience more or less the same world: we have engaged in actions that result in similar, if not identical, impressions of what the world is like.

In addition to this general karma, there is also individual karma, which accounts for the particular variations in the experience of each and every being. To be greedy or to steal establishes a tendency which, if reinforced, results in experiences of poverty and want, often in a future lifetime. On the other hand, to be generous, materially or otherwise, establishes conditions which, if reinforced, result in prosperity. Deliberate acts of killing establish a tendency which, if reinforced, results in a great deal of sickness and shortness of life, whereas to protect and respect life is conducive to good health and longevity. In short, while human beings share general qualities that are common to the human condition, some are richer or poorer than others, happier or unhappier, healthier or unhealthier, longer or shorter lived.

So, karma has both general and specific aspects, which together account for our group and individual experience. To understand the nature of that experience, however, and how the karmic process of cause and effect works, we have to understand the nature of mind. To understand the nature of mind and to attain direct experience of it . . . we have to meditate.

In Mahamudra practice, there is an advanced level of realization called . . . "one taste." At this point, the sameness of subject and object becomes apparent, and causality becomes empirically obvious. We can see a given cause leading to a given effect.

—Kalu Rinpoche, *The Dharma: That Illuminates All Beings Impartially Like the Light of the Sun and the Moon*

SAMSARA

Everything we experience, all the ups and downs of our life, is fundamentally encapsulated in the word *samsara*. Samsara is a wheel that is endlessly spinning. We think that life progresses in a straight line pointed in the direction of improvement, but in fact, we're in a circle of illusion that keeps us ending up just where we started. Karma, the action of cause and effect, is what keeps us here. No matter who we are, we're caught in this process.

Samsara always has to have the last word. We need one more thing to make us happy. One thing leads to the next, perpetuated by our desire to have final satisfaction. But the next experience feels uneasy, and we still need one more thing. We need to eat, then we need to listen to music, then we need to watch a movie, then we need to relax in a bath. The desire to feel satisfied is a continual process that drives our lives, and the end result is suffering. Samsara is not a sin; it's just what ends up happening when we're driven by negative emotions. What ends up happening is called suffering. From the perspective of the Buddha, we keep ourselves on this wheel lifetime after lifetime.

. . .

If we plant peaches, we're always going to get peaches. If we plant pears, we're always going to get pears. Karma works in just this way. If you plant nonvirtue . . . you get suffering. If you plant virtue . . . you get happiness. If we're using strong negative emotions to get what we want, and what we want is happiness, it's never going to work. Therefore we need to contemplate our intentions and actions. Contemplating samsara and karma strengthens our intention to point our life away from suffering and toward true happiness.

—Sakyong Mipham, *Turning the Mind into an Ally*

KARMA MEANS . . .

Karma means you don't get away with nothing.

—Ruth Denison, oral teaching, Dhammadena Retreat

ENLIGHTENMENT AND THE
BODHISATTVA PATH

BECOMING ENLIGHTENED

Before becoming enlightened you just think that you are here and things that are not you are over there, and you are unable to take even one step out of a dualistic world. Experience enlightenment, even shallow enlightenment, and you naturally understand that the thought of "objects over there" is completely mistaken—you have opened your eyes on a world where the totality is yourself. This is enlightenment.

Just to understand that oneself and others are the same is not yet complete enlightenment. As it says in the poem . . . "To encounter the absolute is not yet enlightenment." To experience that all ten directions of the world are the whole body of your Self is enlightenment.

—Taizan Maezumi in *The Hazy Moon of Enlightenment:*
Part of the On Zen Practice Collection,
by Taizan Maezumi and Bernie Glassman

NO ONE BORN

Hey, listen. There's no one here, just this. No owner, no one to be old, to be young, to be good or bad, weak or strong. Just this, that's all; various elements of nature playing themselves out, all empty. No one born and no one to die. Those who speak of death are speaking the language of ignorant children. In the language of the heart, of Dharma, there's no such thing.

When we carry a burden, it's heavy. When there's no one to carry it, there's not a problem in the world. Do not look for good or bad or for anything at all. Do not be anything. There's nothing more; just this.

—Ajahn Chah in *A Still Forest Pool: The Insight Meditation of Achaan Chah*, by Jack Kornfield and Paul Breiter

THE TIMELESS BUDDHA

We take refuge in Buddha, Dharma, and Sangha. . . . What is this Buddha? When we see with the eye of wisdom, we know that the Buddha is timeless, unborn, unrelated to any body, any history, any image. Buddha is the ground of all being, the realization of the truth of the unmoving mind.

So the Buddha was not enlightened in India. In fact, he was never enlightened, was never born, and never died. This timeless Buddha is our true home, our abiding place.

—Ajahn Chah in *A Still Forest Pool: The Insight Meditation of Achaan Chah*, by Jack Kornfield and Paul Breiter

THE BIRTH OF FREEDOM

The impulse to be free is actually coming directly from a freedom that is already starting to break into consciousness. The evolution is going from misunderstanding, which is ignorance, to Wisdom, which is Self realization. The impulse to be free comes from Wisdom.

—Adyashanti, *The Impact of Awakening: Excerpts from the Teachings of Adyashanti*

NIRVANA

The word *nirvana* . . . means extinction of thirst and the annihilation of suffering. Buddhist masters teach that within each of us there is always a fire. Sometimes this fire is quietly smoldering; other times it is raging out of control. This fire is caused by the friction of duality rubbing against itself, like two sticks. This friction is generated by me (as subject) wanting other (as object) and the interaction between the two. This ever-present friction that irritates us blazes up into the fires of suffering. When we realize emptiness and perfect oneness with all, the fires of duality go out. When even the embers themselves are cool, when conflicting emotions are no longer burning us—this is nirvana, the end of dissatisfaction and suffering. This is liberation; this is bliss; this is true freedom.

The freedom from craving spoken of by the Buddha is an inconceivable inner peace, a sense of at-one-ness and completion.

The lasting happiness the Buddha speaks of does not mean having no personality or passion. Desirelessness means lacking nothing. Consider this possibility . . . for your life.

—Lama Surya Das, *Awakening the Buddha Within: Tibetan Wisdom for the Western World*

NATURAL EASE

Above all, be at ease, be as natural and spacious as possible. Slip quietly out of the noose of your habitual anxious self, release all grasping, and relax into your true nature. Think of your ordinary, emotional, thought-ridden self as a block of ice or a slab of butter left out in the sun. If you are feeling hard and cold, let this aggression melt away in the sunlight of your meditation. Let peace work on you and enable you to gather your scattered mind . . . and awaken in you the awareness and insight of Clear Seeing. And you will find all your negativity disarmed, your aggression dissolved, and your confusion evaporating slowly like mist into the vast and stainless sky of your absolute nature.

—Sogyal Rinpoche, *The Tibetan Book of Living and Dying*

EVERYDAY NIRVANA

The sphere of *nirvana*, which means coolness, is something that naturally exists for people to attain. It is like precious medicine which can extinguish all kinds of suffering. Indeed, suffering or disease exists, and no ordinary medicine can ever relieve it. This is the disease caused by the entanglements of greed, anger, and delusion which must be cured with the extinction of the defilements that leads to the condition of nirvana. This sickness is the utmost ailment of the soul, hidden secretly in us and secretly tormenting us. Whoever extinguishes it will be the person who reaches the pinnacle of being human.

To say that there is no nirvana in the present time is absolutely wrong, because the nirvana condition is ever present in nature. If we just behave as truly right-minded followers, nirvana will appear, because it has been waiting for those in search of it.

Anyone can see that if grasping and aversion were with us all day and night without ceasing, who could ever stand them? Under that condition, living things would either die or become insane. Instead, we survive because there are natural periods of coolness, of wholeness and ease. In fact, they last longer than the fires of our grasping and fear. It is this that sustains us. We have periods of rest making us refreshed, alive, and well. Why don't we feel thankful for this everyday nirvana?

—Buddhadhasa Bikkhu, "Everyday Nirvana"

THE END OF TROUBLE

Nirvana, the end of all our troubles, the extinction of [the] fire of craving, is just on the other side of each moment of craving, of hanging on. That's where the great "letting go" comes in and must take place. Then ultimate peace is right there; total fulfillment, wholeness, the end of all craving, luminous and profound; simple not complicated, unfathomable, bottomless, yet inexhaustibly rich. Not like those little thought bubbles we are always trying to collect so that at least we have something to show for ourselves— a whole pile of little thought bubbles on a pad, big deal! Is that all we shall have at the sunset of our lives, a big, frothy pile of foam?

—Lama Surya Das, *Awakening the Buddha Within: Tibetan Wisdom for the Western World*

THE WAY TO NIRVANA

When people ask, "Where is nirvana? Can people still reach nirvana these days?" I answer, "Nirvana is here and now."

Nirvana is everywhere. It dwells in no particular place. It can only be found in the present moment. It is in the mind.

Nirvana is the absence of suffering. It is empty and void of concept. Nothing can compromise nirvana. Nirvana is beyond cause and effect. Nirvana is the highest happiness. It is absolute peace. Peace in the world depends on conditions, but peace in nirvana is unchanging.

In nirvana there is no clinging, no expectation, and no desire. Each moment is fresh, new, and innocent.

All your suffering leads the way to nirvana. When you truly understand suffering, you become free.

—Maha Ghosananda, *Step by Step:*
Meditations on Wisdom and Compassion

THE TRUTH LIBERATES

When the mind is still silent, not seeking anything, it is possible to see what is true.

And it is the truth that liberates, not your efforts to be free.

—J. Krishnamurti, source unknown

DELUSION AND ENLIGHTENMENT

When he achieved enlightenment, Shakyamuni Buddha said, "How wonderful, how wonderful! How truly miraculous! All sentient beings have the wisdom and virtue of the Tathagatha."

That is, everything, just as it is, is fully enlightened. We just can't see it, just can't accept it. And why not? Because we're deluded. And what are these delusions? How can it be that at the very same time that we are completely enlightened, that we are the Buddha, we are also deluded? In this room there are thirty or forty people, and there are at least thirty or forty different types of delusions, and thirty or forty Buddhas.

—Taizan Maezumi in *The Hazy Moon of Enlightenment:*
Part of the On Zen Practice Collection,
by Taizan Maezumi and Bernie Glassman

NO OTHER SHORE

You only arrive at the other shore when you finally realize that there is no other shore. In other words, we make a journey to the "promised land," the other shore, and we have arrived when we realize that we were there all along. It is very paradoxical.

—Chögyam Trungpa,
Cutting Through Spiritual Materialism

UNMOVED

There's a point when you intuitively realize that to be Free you have to give up your attachment to Freedom. You have to quit asking yourself: Is it still there? Am I okay? You have to decide to never look over your shoulder again to see if you're Free or if others know you're Free. You just have to let yourself burn there—no matter what.

In the beginning, teachers can help a lot. But the deeper you go, all they can do is point, and clarify, and tell you what you need to do. Only you can take this step. Nobody can push you into this place.

It's like Buddha's final night under the Bodhi tree. What did he do when confronted with this? He reached down and touched the ground and said, "I will not be moved." Finally—when everything that could be thrown at him was thrown, and he was still unmoved—it was done. He never looked back.

> —Adyashanti, *The Impact of Awakening:*
> *Excerpts from the Teachings of Adyashanti*

TURN TOWARD CONSCIOUSNESS

There is a clear distinction between consciousness itself and the transient states that arise within it. All experiences are merely conditioned states. Through not understaning we take them to be real, when in fact they are just transient. Do not seek after them. Turn your attention to consciousness itself and become (*sikkhibbuto*) a witness to this truth. When the true nature of conscioiusness is seen, then you can stop, you can put all things down and rest. There's nothing more to do than this.

—Ajahn Mun, adapted from *Food for the Heart: The Collected Teachings of Ajahn Chah* by Ajahn Chah

NO NEED TO STRUGGLE

There is no need to struggle to be free; the absence of struggle is in itself freedom.

—Chögyam Trungpa,
Cutting Through Spiritual Materialism

THE DHARMA IS EVERYWHERE

It doesn't matter where you are.
The dharma is everywhere.

—Dipa Ma in *Knee Deep in Grace:*
The Extraordinary Life and Teaching of Dipa Ma,
by Amy Schmidt

[218]

THE PURE HEART SHINES

Whenever identification with greed, fear, and confusion drops away, we see that the heart is clear and open. This is its natural state. This spacious openness or pure consciousness is Enlightenment. Relax, and let go and you can taste it here and now. Do not be confused because the various traditions describe enlightenment differently, as peace or love. When you experience pure consciousness, you find it has many beautiful qualities. In this, it is like a diamond crystal. One facet of pure consciousness is vast silence, another is perfect peace, another is luminous clarity, and another is boundless love. Pure consciousness is all of these qualities, joy, perfection, compassion, and freedom. It is timeless, radiant, blissful, ever present, infinitely creative, completely empty, and full of all things. No need to grasp any form or description. Let go of striving. Open the gate. Experience the joy of freedom now.

—Jack Kornfield, adapted from *The Wise Heart:*
A Guide to the Universal Teachings of Buddhist Psychology

BEING THE BUDDHA

I used to meet people, and I'd visualize how they could be, and my desire to have them change made me look into their eyes and touch them in a certain way, and they'd start to be who I wanted them to be. Then I'd say, "Look at that," and they'd say, "Oh, thank you, thank you." And they'd love me and want to follow me around. But the next day or week or month they'd come down because they were living out of my mind, not theirs. They were living out my desire of how they ought to be, not being how in fact they needed to be in their own journey of evolution. The best we can do is become an environment for every person we meet that allows them to open in the optimum way they can open. The way you "raise" a child is to create a space with your own love and consciousness to allow that child to become what it must become in this lifetime.

It's the same if we're therapists or marriage partners or spiritual teachers; whatever our roles in human relationships, the game is always the same. If you're a policeman on traffic duty, your job may be to give people traffic tickets. How you give a traffic ticket is a function of your evolution. You can give a person a traffic ticket in such a way that they'd end up enlightened—because there is no form to this game at all. It's who's in the form that counts. It isn't how holy we look; it's how much we *are* the spirit of the living Christ, the compassion of the Buddha, the love of Krishna, the fierce discriminating wisdom of Tara or Kali. There isn't even one action or emotion that's holier than any other. People get into thinking one form of emotional action is more holy. For example, when Maharaj-ji said to me, "Ram Dass, give up anger." And I said, "Well, Maharaj-ji, can't I even use anger as a teaching device?' And he said angrily, "No!"

—Ram Dass, *Grist for the Mill*

EACH PERSON'S PATH

There is no form that in and of itself is closer to God. All forms are just forms . . . not better to stay single or to marry; not better to marry or to stay single. Each individual has his or her unique karmic predicament; each individual must therefore listen very carefully to hear her or his dharma or way or path. For one person it will be as a mother, or for another it will be Brahmachary or celibate. For one it will be to be a householder, for another to be a saddhu, a wandering monk. Not better or worse. To live another's dharma, to try to be Buddha or to be Christ because Christ did it, doesn't get us there; it just makes us mimickers. This game is much more subtle; we have to listen to hear what our path through is, moment by moment, choice by choice.

—Ram Dass, *Grist for the Mill*

SWEEP LIKE MICHELANGELO

If a person sweeps streets for a living, they should sweep like Raphael painted pictures, like Michelangelo carved marble, like Shakespeare wrote poetry, like Beethoven composed music.

—Martin Luther King Jr.
"What Is Your Life's Blueprint?"

STAY WHERE YOU ARE

Wouldn't it be sweet to come home and find the Buddha there, simply and utterly at peace, desireless with a hearty warmth and genuine nobility of spirit? Wouldn't it be satisfying to be like that, to be in touch with your own authentic being? That's why an Indian master, when asked what advice he had for Westerners seeking enlightenment, said, "Stay where you are." A statement that is simple, yet profound. Be wherever you are; be whoever you are. When *you* genuinely become *you,* a Buddha realizes Buddhahood. You become a Buddha by actualizing your own original innate nature. This nature is primordially pure. This is your true nature, your natural mind. This innate Buddha-nature doesn't need to achieve enlightenment because it is always already perfect, from the beginningless beginning. We only have to awaken to it. There is nothing more to seek or look for.

—Lama Surya Das, *Awakening the Buddha Within: Tibetan Wisdom for the Western World*

REALIZATION IS THE EASY PART

Always the realization is the easy part. Actualizing the realization is the hard part, which is why we say it takes ten, twenty, thirty, forty, fifty years of practice to know what enlightenment is, to really know what it is in the bones and the marrow. When Hakuin Zenji was in his seventies, having had maybe a dozen major enlightenment experiences and innumerable minor ones, he said that he was finally getting to the point where his body was acting in accord with the way that he saw things. We practice, and in a way we can say there's no need to practice. The cushion's the cushion. I am what I am. But that's not enough. Thank you.

—Taizan Maezumi, *The Hazy Moon of Enlightenment*

TASTE AND ZEST

There is so much sameness in ordinary life. We are always experiencing everything through the same set of lenses. Once greed, hatred, and delusion are gone, you see everything fresh and new all the time. Every moment is new. Life was dull before. Now, every day, every moment is full of taste and zest.

—Dipa Ma in *Knee Deep in Grace:*
The Extraordinary Life and Teaching of Dipa Ma,
by Amy Schmidt

HOME COOKING

When I first started cooking at Tassajara, I had a problem. I could not get my biscuits to come out right. I'd follow the recipe and try variations . . . but nothing worked. I had in mind the "perfect" biscuit, and these just didn't measure up.

Growing up, I had "made" two kinds of biscuits: one was from Bisquick and the other from Pillsbury. For the Bisquick biscuits, you added milk to the mix and then blobbed the dough in spoonfuls onto the pan—you didn't even need to roll them out. The biscuits from Pillsbury came in a kind of cardboard can. You rapped the can on the corner of the counter and it popped open. Then you twisted the can open more, put the premade biscuits on a pan and baked them. I really liked those Pillsbury biscuits. Isn't that what biscuits should taste like? Mine just weren't coming out the way they were supposed to.

It's wonderful and amazing the ideas we get about what biscuits should taste like, or what a life should look like. Compared to what? Canned biscuits from Pillsbury? *"Leave it to Beaver?* . . .

People who ate my biscuits could be extolling their virtues, eating one after another, but for me, [those perfectly good] biscuits were not "right."

Finally one day that shifting-into-place occurred, an awakening: not "right" compared to what? Oh, no! I've been trying to make canned Pillsbury biscuits! Then that exquisite moment of actually tasting my biscuits without comparing them to some (previously hidden) standard: wheaty, flaky, buttery, sunny, earthy, here. Inconceivably delicious, incomparably alive, present, vibrant. In fact, much more satisfying than any memory. . . . Those moments—when you realize your life as it is is just fine, thank you—can be so stunning and liberating. Only the insidious comparison to a beautifully prepared, beautifully packaged product makes it seem insufficient. The effort to produce a life with no dirty bowls, no messy feelings, no depression, no anger is bound to fail—and be endlessly frustrating. Then savoring, actually tasting the present moment of experience—how much more complex and multifaceted. How unfathomable. . . .

As a Zen student one can spend years trying to make it look right, trying to cover the faults, conceal the messes. Everyone knew what the Bisquick Zen student looked like: calm, buoyant, cheerful, energetic, deep, profound. Our motto, as one of my friends says, was, "Looking good."

We've all done it . . . tried to look good as a husband, wife, or parent. . . .

Well, to heck with it, I say, wake up and smell the coffee— and how about savoring some good old home cooking, the biscuits of today?

—Ed Brown, *The Complete Tassajara Cookbook: Recipes, Techniques, and Reflections from the Famed Zen Kitchen*

ONE HEART GRACE

As we make ready to eat this food
we remember with gratitude
the many people, tools, animals and plants,
air and water, sky and earth,
turned in the wheel of living and dying,
whose joyful exertion
provide our sustenance this day. May we with the
blessing of this food
join our hearts
to the one heart of the world
in awareness and love,
and may we together with everyone
realize the path of awakening,
and never stop making effort
for the benefit of others.

—Norman Fischer, Everydayzen.org

TRUTH TELLING

I believe we are obliged to tell the truth. Telling the truth is a way we take care of people. The Buddha taught complete honesty, with the extra instruction that everything a person says should be truthful *and* helpful

When the Buddha taught Right Speech, he provided a guide for making corrections. Admonitions, he said, should be timely, truthful, gentle, kind, and helpful. When I tell people those criteria, they often exclaim, "But then no one could ever admonish anyone!" I think otherwise. I think with Right Speech people can make suggestions or observations in a way that the other person can hear and use them without feeling diminished.

—Sylvia Boorstein, *It's Easier Than You Think: The Buddhist Way to Happiness*

ALIGN YOUR HEART

What difference would it make in your life if you engaged the world with a conscious commitment to end sorrow or pain wherever you meet it? What difference would it make to wake in the morning and greet your family, the stranger beside you on the bus, the troublesome colleague, with the intention to listen to them wholeheartedly and be present for them? Compassion doesn't always call for grand or heroic gestures. It asks you to find in your heart the simple but profound willingness to be present, with a commitment to end sorrow and contribute to the well-being and ease of all beings. A word of kindness, a loving touch, a patient presence, a willingness to step beyond your fears and reactions are all gestures of compassion that can transform a moment of fear or pain. Aligning yourself with the path of understanding and compassion, you are learning to listen to the cries of the world.

The universe is full of beings, those you know and those who will forever be strangers. The world is made up of those you care for, those you are indifferent to, and those you fear or dislike. With those you love and care for, your compassion is often unhesitating: you reach out to console, support, and encourage without reservation. With those who are strangers, your response may vary. You may feel an indifference that you are ashamed of or a vague sympathy that is quickly forgotten in the busyness of your life. With those you dislike, your compassion for their suffering can be subtly mixed with an embarrassed satisfaction over their suffering. Compassion is an invitation to cross the divide that separates "us" from "them." At times these almost imperceptible barriers are lifted. You see lines of pain in the faces of refugees or the homeless woman on the street, and your heart trembles. You listen again to the anguish of the person you resent and find that your history of struggle with him is released, as the hardness of your heart begins to soften. Suddenly you are present in a new way—free of prejudice and fear. It is as if your heart has expanded, revealing all of life as one organism.

—Christina Feldman, *Compassion:*
Listening to the Cries of the World

GATHA FOR ALL
THREATENED BEINGS

Ah Power that swirls us together
Grant us Bliss
Grant us the great release
And to all Beings
Vanishing, wounded
In trouble on earth,
We pass on this love
May their numbers increase

—Gary Snyder, *Left Out in the Rain: Poems*

THE REAL PEACE

Peace, in the sense of absence of war, is of little value to someone who is dying of hunger or cold. It will not remove the pain of torture inflicted on a prisoner of conscience. It does not comfort those who have lost their loved ones in floods caused by senseless deforestation in a neighboring country. Peace can only last where human rights are respected, where the people are fed, and where individuals and nations are free. True peace with oneself and with the world around us can only be achieved through the development of mental peace.

—The Dalai Lama,
The Essential Dalai Lama: His Important Teachings

SAVE THE EARTH

Our personal attempts to live humanely in this world are never wasted. Choosing to cultivate love rather than anger just might be what it takes to save the planet from extinction.

—Pema Chödrön, *The Places That Scare You:
A Guide to Fearlessness in Difficult Times*

THE ETERNAL LAW OF LOVE

Once, I was working with a friend and teacher, Maha Ghosananda, the "Gandhi of Cambodia." He was one of the few monastics to survive the Cambodian genocide, and in response, he decided to open a Buddhist temple in a barren refugee camp filled with Khmer Rouge communists. In the hot and crowded camp were fifty thousand villagers who had become communists at gunpoint and had now fled to the Thai border. When the bamboo temple was nearly finished, the Khmer Rouge underground threatened to kill any who went there. In spite of this, a temple gong was rung, and on its opening day, more than twenty thousand people crowded into the dusty square for the ceremony. Now in front of him were the sad remnants of other broken families; an uncle with two nieces, a mother with only one of three children. Their schools had been burned, their villages destroyed, and in nearly every family, members had been executed or ripped away. Their faces were filled with sorrow. All of Maha Ghosananda's family had been killed. I wondered what he would say to people who had suffered so greatly.

Maha Ghosananda began the service with the traditional chants that had permeated village life for a thousand years. Though these words had been silenced for years and the temples destroyed, they still remained in the hearts of these people whose lives had known as much sorrow and injustice as any on earth.

Then Maha Ghosananda began chanting one of the central teachings of the Buddha, first in Pali and then in Cambodian, reciting the words over and over:

> Hatred never ceases by hatred
> but by love alone is healed.
> This is the ancient and eternal law.

As he chanted these verses over and over, hundreds, then thousands began to chant with him. They chanted and wept. These were the tears of the Dharma falling on their parched hearts, for it was clear that the truth of this chant and their longing for forgiveness was even greater than the sorrows they had to bear.

—Jack Kornfield and Christina Feldman, adapted from
Soul Food: Stories to Nourish the Spirit and the Heart

COMPASSION IN ACTION

Compassion in action is paradoxical and mysterious. It is absolute yet continually changing. It accepts that everything is happening exactly as it should, and it works with a full-hearted commitment to change. It sets goals but knows that the process is all there is. It is joyful in the midst of suffering and hopeful in the face of overwhelming odds. It is simple in a world of complexity and confusion. It is done for others, but it nurtures the self. It shields in order to be strong. It intends to eliminate suffering, knowing that suffering is limitless. It is action arising from emptiness

—Ram Dass in *Compassion in Action:*
Setting Out on the Path of Service,
by Ram Dass and Mirabai Bush

SITTING FOR PEACE

After the Gulf War had been going on for two weeks, [I decided to sit for peace every day in the Santa Fe plaza]. A young writer, Rob Wilder . . . heard about it and said he'd like to join me. . . . He had never sat prior to the plaza sittings, but his commitment was true. I got in position, and we sat. It rained that noon, hard. Rob and I were the only ones there. No pigeons, no casual passersby. I watched the rain hit the sidewalk and bounce. My hair was sopping wet, so was my jacket. I was happy to be there, that beautiful, peaceful half hour in the middle of the day. "Make positive effort for the good," [Katagiri] Roshi told me after my divorce. Every day Rob and I were doing that. No matter how crazy I felt in the morning, stirred by the last night's dream or my morning's writing, everything turned when I sat on that zafu outside under trees and sky. I watched how big time was: A half hour was tremendous. How long it took—I could hear the shoe steps—for a person to walk from the statue to the street, across my path. How enormous the rain was with its small hands.

When I met Joan, the realtor, at one, she said, "You

know, while you sat, I went and had a bowl of soup. I never stop in the middle of my day to eat. It was really nice. Thanks." We both smiled.

There were days when one or two of the Santa Fe crazies who hang out on the plaza joined us. One sat next to Rob with the big boom box on his lap blasting, "I left my Chevy on the levee," and trying to talk to me. I sat still. Should I say something? In a moment, I turned to him: "We're silent now. Later we'll talk." I turned my head back. He sat a few moments more and then wandered off. One man sat still for ten minutes, said, "Man, I can't do this any longer," left, and returned at the end for five minutes. Two tourists, who didn't know each other, sat down at 12:05. The woman from New York began a discussion about peace with the man. She gave her precise opinion of the Vietnam War. Again, I turned. "We can talk later. Please let's just sit now."

"Oh, I can't do that," and she trailed off. The man scratched his ear and followed her. An old man with a wool hat said one day, "I'll show you how to get real peace," and he handed us a photocopied page from the Bible.

Three secretaries brought lunches and sat on a bench across from us and discussed their boss. "Oh, I saw a bottle in his lower left-hand drawer." They giggled.

Many times Rob and I sat alone. One day it snowed. The pigeons looked beautiful through the white flakes.

There was a fat gray one that always seemed to lag behind and miss the thrown popcorn. He scurried to another place and was shut out there, too.

And one day it seemed to bubble up from the very earth I sat on—I heard Roshi's words. Words he'd repeated often in his lectures, but that I had paid little attention to before. Now I heard them: "Peace is not a matter of discussion. Shut up and, like the Buddha, sit down under the old tree." Peace is not something to fight over. I heard his words. I heard them. He was with me again. In my ribs and chest and lungs and face and hair. I carried him in me. He was sitting with me and with the trees and birds. It was so simple.

—Natalie Goldberg, *Long Quiet Highway: Waking Up in America*

TRUTH AND LOVE HAVE ALWAYS WON

When I despair, I remember that all through history, the way of truth and love has always won. There have been tyrants and murderers, and for a time, they can seem invincible. But in the end, they always fall. Think of it—always.

—Mahatma Gandhi in *Gandhi,*
screenplay by John Briley

THE UNITY OF ALL

I believe in the unity of all things, and I believe that if one person gains the whole world gains, and if one person falls the whole world falls to that extent.

—Mahatma Gandhi in *True Patriotism:*
Some Sayings of Mahatma Gandhi,
edited by S. Hobhouse

SMALL IS BEAUTIFUL: ECONOMICS
AS IF PEOPLE MATTERED

While the materialist is mainly interested in good, the Buddhist is mainly interested in liberation. But Buddhism is "The Middle Way" and therefore in no way antagonistic to physical well-being. It is not wealth that stands in the way of liberation but the attachment to wealth; not the enjoyment of pleasurable things but the craving for them. The keynote of Buddhist economics, therefore, is simplicity and non-violence. From an economist's point of view, the marvel of the Buddhist way of life is the utter rationality of its pattern—amazingly small means leading to extraordinarily satisfactory results.

For the modern economist, this is very difficult to understand. He is used to measuring the "standard of living" by the amount of annual consumption, assuming all the time that a man who consumes more is "better off" than a man who consumes less. A Buddhist economist would consider this approach excessively irrational: since consumption is merely a means to human well-being, the aim should be to obtain the maximum of well-being with the minimum of consumption. Thus, if the purpose of clothing is a certain amount of temperature, comfort, and an attractive appearance, the task is to attain this purpose with the smallest possible effort, that is, with the smallest annual destruction of cloth and with the help of designs that involve the smallest possible input of toil. The less toil there is, the more time and strength is left for artistic creativity. It would be highly uneconomic, for instance, to go in for complicated tailoring, like the modern West, when a much more beautiful effect can be achieved by the skillful draping of uncut material. It would be the height of folly to make material so that it should wear out quickly and the height of barbarity to make anything ugly, shabby, or mean. What has just been said about clothing applies equally to all other human requirements. The ownership and consumption of goods is a means to an end, and Buddhist economics is the systematic study of how to attain given ends with the minimum means.

—E. F. Schumacher, *Small Is Beautiful: Economics as if People Mattered*

ENORMOUS POWER

Each of us has enormous power.
It can be used to help ourselves and help others.

—Dipa Ma in *Knee Deep in Grace:*
*The Extraordinary Life and Teaching of Dipa M*a,
by Amy Schmidt

THE PILLARS OF DHARMA

The One Dharma of Western Buddhism emerges as a grand tapestry of teachings, weaving together from different traditions the methods of mindfulness, the motivation of compassion, and the liberating wisdom of nonclinging. These three pillars—mindfulness, compassion, and wisdom—are not Indian or Burmese, Japanese or Tibetan; they are qualities in our own minds. Multiple paths illuminate these qualities, and many practices enhance their growth. From the first moments of self-awareness to the full flowering of *Bodhicitta*, teachings from different traditions inspire, instruct, and lead us to that place where we may truly be of benefit to all.

The practice of mindfulness has the potential to transform our society. We see the beginnings of this in the work of mindfulness-based stress-reduction programs now spreading throughout the country. We see it in the mindfulness training of athletes and sports teams. We see it in programs offering contemplative mindfulness practices to groups of businesspeople, lawyers, journalists, environmental activists, scholars, and philanthropists. Most of all, we see it in the growing interest among people of all ages for periods of silent retreat. In the increased busyness and distractedness of our lives, there is a strong need for the quiet transforming beauty of silence and awareness. It is from the depth of mindfulness practice, as well as its breadth, that realization happens and that awakening to wisdom becomes a treasured value of our society.

As we integrate mindfulness into the world, compassion increasingly becomes the expression of our spiritual path. It manifests in small, individual ways and also as larger trends in our culture. An evolving collaboration of practitioners who seek to actively engage with the suffering in the world has inspired what is called "engaged Buddhism." This movement draws strength both from the Buddhist teachings on *Bodhicitta*, which remind us that practice is not for ourselves alone but for the welfare and happiness of all beings, and from the deep wellsprings of social action found within the Western Judeo-Christian tradition. Compassion and care for the world provide common ground in the many interreligious dialogues now taking place. These exchanges are slowly breaking down barriers of isolation, suspicion, and sectarianism among practitioners of various schools and religions.

The essence of One Dharma is wisdom. We practice paying attention—to our bodies, our thoughts, our emotions, to awareness itself—and through a deepening concentration and stillness of mind, we gain insight into some basic truths. Wisdom sees the impermanent, ephemeral nature of experience and the fundamental unreliability of changing phenomena. Wisdom opens our minds to selflessness, the great liberating jewel of the Buddha's enlightenment, and to the clear recognition of the Nature of Mind: intrinsically empty, naturally radiant, ceaselessly responsive. Finally, wisdom brings the understanding that nonclinging is the essential unifying experience of freedom. We see that nonclinging is both a practice to cultivate and the nature of the awakened mind itself.

—Joseph Goldstein, *One Dharma:*
The Emerging Western Buddhism

THE HUMAN GATE

The greatest lesson I have learned is that the universal must be wedded to our immediate personal circumstances to be fulfilled in spiritual life. The human gate to the sacred is our own body, heart, and mind, our history and the closest relationships and circumstances of our life. If not here, where else could we bring alive compassion, justice, and liberation?

We must first begin with ourselves. The universal truths of spiritual life can come alive only in our personal circumstance. This personal approach to practice honors the timeless and mysterious dance of birth and death, and also our particular body, our particular family and community, the personal history and the joys and sorrows that have been given to us. In this way, our awakening is a very personal matter that also affects all other creatures on earth.

—Jack Kornfield, adapted from *A Path with Heart: A Guide through the Perils and Promises of Spiritual Life*

RELIGION AND POLITICS

To see the universal and all-pervading Spirit of Truth face to face, one must be able to love the meanest of creation as oneself. And a man who aspires after that cannot afford to keep out of any field of life. That is why my devotion to Truth has drawn me into the field of politics; and I can say without the slightest hesitation, and yet in all humility, that those who say that religion has nothing to do with politics do not know what religion means.

—Mahatma Gandhi, *Gandhi: An Autobiography:*
The Story of My Experiments with Truth

CLEANSING OUR PERCEPTIONS

The other day the little stream that runs near the center was gushing noisily downhill with lots of muddy water hiding its depth. Today it is flowing quietly, clearly, exposing sheets of brightly shimmering green bedrock.

Can we see things just as they are right now? Without wanting them to be otherwise? Without comparing them favorably or unfavorably? Without wanting them to stay this way forever? Without clinging and depending? Without wanting to own and possess?

Can we human beings share life on earth together without trying to own each other or trying to get rid of each other? The idea of possessing each other gives an illusory sense of security. Along with it inevitably goes the fear of losing what we have become accustomed and attached to.

What does it mean to see each other exactly as we are? Past memories about ourselves and each other are *not* what we are right now. Memory is an incomplete and inaccurate recording of the past. Now is something entirely different.

Quietly looking and listening *now* is not memory. It is an entirely different mode of mind. It is a cleansing of perception.

—Toni Packer, *The Work of This Moment*

A UNIVERSE OF
INTERCONNECTEDNESS

As long as we remain on the surface of life, everyone and everything seems to exist as isolated entities. But when we look below the surface, we see strata upon strata of dynamic interconnectedness. If we look to the greatest depth, Buddhism says, we will see a world where no one and no thing stands apart.

A plate of spaghetti for dinner, for instance, isn't just a jumble of noodles to which we add tomato sauce. Those noodles have emerged out of someone's labor in growing the wheat, their hopes and fears and dreams for their children, the soil and air and rainfall and sunlight that nurtured and supported the growth of that crop. These elements are themselves interactively affected by depletions in the ozone layer and by the loss of the Amazon rain forests, by global warming and by acid rain. A host of environmental degradations, neglectful industries, government regulations, and hopeful interventions are among the conditions giving rise to our plate of spaghetti.

Included in our dinner as well are the efforts of those

who shipped the wheat, and those who milled it, and the shopping we ourselves did the night before at our local neighborhood grocery store, kept open by the young proprietor's fearful obsession with a secure old age. Also included is the culinary history of Italy, where pasta became a staple, as well as that of China, where laborers on vast paddies were among the first to eat noodles.

And still this is just a tiny part of the converging conditions. What about the conditions that affected our childhood food cravings, and then our lifelong eating habits? What about the latest board meeting concerning the advertising budget of the company that enticed us to buy their particular brand of pasta? Looking below the surface, we see revealed a world in which a single plate of spaghetti comes out of an entire universe of interconnectedness.

—Sharon Salzberg, *Faith*

THE GREAT TURNING

Imagine that future generations will look back on these closing years of the twentieth century and call it the time of the Great Turning. It is the epochal shift from an industrial growth society, dependent on accelerating consumption of resources, to a sustainable or life-sustaining society.

Scientists . . . see more quickly than the politicians that there is no technological fix. No magic bullet, not even the Internet, can save us from population explosion, deforestation, continuing racism and warfare, poison by pollution, and wholesale extinctions of plant and animal species. We are going to have to want different things, seek different pleasures, pursue different goals, than those that have been driving us and our global economy.

There is, among people of all faiths, an urgency to taste and know this relatedness and to break down the old dichotomies between self and world, mind and nature, contemplation and action. Perhaps we suspect that our survival depends upon our doing that.

—Joanna Macy, "The Great Turning:
Reflections on Our Moment in History"
and *World as Lover, World as Self*

THE WEB OF LIFE

The way we define and delimit the self is arbitrary. We can place it between our ears and have it looking out from our eyes; or we can widen it to include the air we breathe, or, at other moments, we can cast its boundaries farther to include the oxygen-giving trees and plankton, our external lungs, and beyond them the web of life in which they are sustained.

To experience the world as an extended self and its story as our own extended story involves no surrender or eclipse of our individuality.

Basic to most spiritual traditions, as well as the systems view of the world, is the recognition that we are not separate, isolated entities, but integral and organic parts of the vast web of life. As such, we are like neurons in a neural net, through which flow currents of awareness of what is happening to us, as a species and as a planet. In that context, the pain we feel for our world is a living testimony to our interconnectedness with it. If we deny this pain, we become like blocked and atrophied neurons, deprived of life's flow and weakening the larger body in which we take being. But if we let it move through us, we affirm our belonging; our collective awareness increases. We can open to the pain of the world in confidence that it can neither shatter nor isolate us, for we are not objects that can break. We are resilient patterns within a vaster web of knowing.

Because we have been conditioned to view ourselves as separate, competitive, and thus fragile entities, it takes practice to relearn this kind of resilience. A good way to begin is by practicing simple openness, as in the exercise of "breathing through," adapted from an ancient Buddhist meditation for the development of compassion.

—Joanna Macy, *World as Lover, World as Self*

BEYOND OUR HABIT

Instead of always imposing our habitual viewpoint onto things, it can help to remind ourselves how open the world is to interpretation. For example, looking at a tree, a doctor may see it as a source of medicine or poison. A trader might calculate its monetary value, and a carpenter might measure its construction potential. A scientist might analyze its chemical and electrical impulses. A drunk might see the same tree as a wheel spinning over his head. A poet might lose herself in its beauty. A Christian might utter a prayer in praise of God's creation. A Buddhist might see the tree as a manifestation of interdependent causation or an expression of ultimate peace.

Broadening our view can loosen our grasping at self and allow us to realize how our own mental fabrications and habits obscure our peaceful nature.

—Tulku Thondup, *The Healing Power of Mind: Simple Meditation Exercises for Health, Well-Being, and Enlightenment*

UNIVERSAL RESPONSIBILITY

The problems we face today—violent conflicts, destruction of nature, poverty, hunger, and so on—are mainly problems created by humans. They can be resolved—but only through human effort, understanding and the development of a sense of brotherhood and sisterhood. To do this, we need to cultivate a universal responsibility for one another and for the planet we share, based on a good heart and awareness.

Now, although I have found my own Buddhist religion helpful in generating love and compassion, I am convinced that these qualities can be developed by anyone, with or without religion. I further believe that all religions pursue the same goals: those of cultivating goodness and bringing happiness to all human beings. Though the means might appear different, the ends are the same.

—The Dalai Lama, *Freedom in Exile:*
The Autobiography of the Dalai Lama

COMMITTED AND BALANCED

By learning to remain balanced in the face of everything experienced inside, one develops detachment towards all that one encounters in external situations as well. However, this detachment is not escapism or indifference to the problems of the world. Those who regularly practice Vipassana become more sensitive to the sufferings of others and do their utmost to relieve suffering in whatever way they can—not with any agitation, but with a mind full of love, compassion, and equanimity. They learn holy indifference—how to be fully committed, fully involved in helping others, while at the same time maintaining balance of mind. In this way they remain peaceful and happy while working for the peace and happiness of others.

This is what the Buddha taught: an art of living. He never established or taught any religion, any "ism." He never instructed those who came to him to practice any rites or rituals, any empty formalities. Instead, he taught them just to observe nature as it is by observing the reality inside. Out of ignorance, we keep reacting in ways which harm ourselves and others. But when wisdom arises—the wisdom of observing reality as it is—this habit of reacting falls away. When we cease to react blindly, then we are capable of real action—action proceeding from a balanced mind, a mind which sees and understands the truth. Such action can only be positive, creative, helpful to ourselves and to others.

—S. N. Goenka, "The Art of Living:
Vipassana Meditation"

WHAT ONE PERSON CAN DO

When the crowded Vietnamese refugee boats met with storms or pirates, if everyone panicked, all would be lost. But if even one person on the boat remained calm and centered, it was enough. It showed the Way for everyone to survive.

—Thich Nhat Hanh, *Being Peace*

THE POLITICS OF ENLIGHTENMENT

It is obvious that the implementation of the politics of enlightenment is the only way to avoid planetary disaster.

All one needs to understand the inner revolution and live the politics of enlightenment are wisdom about one's long-term self-interest, good-humored tolerance of one's own and others' faults, trust in the adequacy of the environment and our fellow beings, and the courage to take up the responsibility of enlightenment.

Buddha is as buddha does. Just be happy. At least act enlightened. Feel enlightened. It is more pleasant, and enlightenment will follow.

—Robert Thurman, *Inner Revolution:*
Life, Liberty, and the Pursuit of Real Happiness

RELAX

I would like to pass on one little bit of advice I give to everyone. Relax. Just relax. Be nice to each other. As you go through your life, simply be kind to people. Try to help them rather than hurt them. Try to get along with them rather than fall out with them. With that, I will leave you, and with all my very best wishes.

—Nyoshul Khenpo in *One Dharma:*
The Emerging Western Buddhism, by Joseph Goldstein

PRACTICE: TAKE THE ONE SEAT

Let your body be seated comfortably in your chair or on your cushion. Take a posture that is stable, erect, and connected with the earth. Sit as the Buddha did on his night of enlightenment, with great dignity and centeredness, sensing your capacity to face anything that arises. Let your eyes close and let your attention turn to your breathing. Let your breath move freely through your body. Let each breath bring a calmness and an ease. As you breathe, sense your capacity to open in body, heart, and mind.

Open your senses, your feelings, your thoughts with loving compassion. Become aware of what feels closed in your body, closed in your heart, closed in your mind. Breathe and make space. Let the space open so that anything may arise. Let the windows of your senses open. Be aware of whatever feelings, images, sounds, and stories show themselves. With kind attention, notice with interest and ease all that presents itself to you.

Continue to feel your steadiness and connectedness to the earth, as if you had taken the one seat in the center of life and opened yourself to an awareness of its dance. As you sit, feel the benefit of balance and peace in your life. Sense your capacity to rest unshakable as the seasons of life change. See how all that arises will pass away. Reflect on how joys and sorrows, pleasant events and unpleasant events, individuals, nations, even civilizations, arise and pass away. Take the one seat of a Buddha and rest with a heart of equanimity and compassion in the center of it all.

Sit this way, dignified and present, for as long as you wish. After some time, still feeling centered and steady, open your eyes. Then let yourself stand up and take some steps, walking with the same centeredness and dignity. Practice sitting and walking in this fashion, sensing your ability to be open, alive, and present with all that arises on this earth.

—Jack Kornfield, adapted from *A Path with Heart:
A Guide through the Perils and Promises of Spiritual Life*

WALKING MEDITATION

Walking meditation can be very enjoyable. We walk slowly, alone or with friends, if possible in some beautiful place. Walking meditation is really to enjoy the walking—walking not in order to arrive, just for walking. The purpose is to be in the present moment and enjoy each step you make. Therefore you have to shake off all worries and anxieties, not thinking of the future, not thinking of the past, just enjoying the present moment. You can take the hand of a child as you walk, as if you are the happiest person on earth. We walk all the time, but usually it is more like running. Our hurried steps print anxiety and sorrow on the earth. If we can take one step in peace, we can take two, three, four, and then five steps for the peace and happiness of humankind.

Our mind darts from one thing to another, like a monkey swinging from branch to branch without stopping to rest. Thoughts have millions of pathways, and we are forever pulled along by them into the world of forgetfulness. If we can transform our walking path into a field for meditation, our feet will take every step in full awareness.

Our breathing will be in harmony with our steps, and our mind will naturally be at ease. Every step we take will reinforce our peace and joy and cause a stream of calm energy to flow through us. Then we can say, "With each step, a gentle wind blows."

The Buddha is often represented by artists as seated on a lotus flower to suggest the peace and happiness he enjoys. Artists also depict lotus flowers blooming under the footsteps of the newly born Buddha. If we take steps without anxiety, in peace and joy, then we, too, will cause a flower to bloom on the earth with every step.

—Thich Nhat Hanh, *Present Moment, Wonderful Moment: Mindfulness Verses for Daily Living*

ACKNOWLEDGMENTS

Deep appreciation to Noelle Oxenhandler, my inspiring and good-natured co-editor for poring through a mountain of contemporary teaching with a wise heart and a keen Dharma eye.

True gratitude for Sara Sparling whose steadfast and kind assistance in all manner of things—tending, typing, and shepherding—helped complete this book and steward a host of Dharma projects for the benefit of so many.

Bows of thanks to Emily Bower, my thoughtful and unflagging Shambhala editor and dedicated curator of Dharma teachings.

Additional thanks to Sam Bercholz, Peter Turner, Katie Keach, and the other fine staff at Shambhala Publications.

Gratitude for the blessings from my Dharma colleagues and friends who inspire, cheer, and buoy me up, and who have the good fortune to share in a long Western Buddhist lineage from Schopenhauer and Whitman and William James and Lama Govinda and Nyanamoli to our gloriously abundant modern Dharma generation.

[273]

BIBLIOGRAPHY

Adyashanti. *The Impact of Awakening: Excerpts from the Teachings of Adyashanti*. Campbell, Calif.: Open Gate Sangha, 2002.

Allione, Tsultrim. *Feeding Your Demons: Ancient Wisdom for Resolving Inner Conflict*. Boston, Mass.: Little, Brown and Co., 2008.

———. *Women of Wisdom*. Ithaca, N.Y.: Snow Lion Publications, 2000.

Anderson, Laurie. "Wild White Horses." In *What Book!?, Buddha Poems from Beat to Hiphop*, edited by Gary Gach. Berkeley, Calif.: Parallax Press, 1998.

Beck, Charlotte Joko. *Nothing Special: Living Zen*. San Francisco, Calif.: HarperSanFrancisco, 1993.

Boorstein, Sylvia. *It's Easier Than You Think: The Buddhist Way to Happiness*. San Francisco, Calif.: HarperSanFrancisco, 1995.

Brach, Tara. *Radical Acceptance: Embracing Your Life with the Heart of a Buddha*. New York: Bantam Dell, 2003.

Brown, Ed Espe. *The Complete Tassajara Cookbook: Recipes, Techniques, and Reflections from the Famed Zen Kitchen*. Boston, Mass.: Shambhala Publications, 2009.

Buddhadhasa Bikkhu. "Everyday Nirvana." Pamphlet from Wat Suan Moke, Thailand, circulated in 1980s.

Chah, Ajahn. *Food for the Heart: The Collected Teachings of Ajahn Chah*. Somerville, Mass.: Wisdom Publications, 2002.

Chödrön, Pema. *The Places That Scare You: A Guide to Fearlessness in Difficult Times*. Boston, Mass.: Shambhala Publications, 2005.

———. *When Things Fall Apart: Heart Advice for Difficult Times*. Boston, Mass.: Shambhala Publications, 2002.

Dalai Lama, The. *The Essential Dalai Lama: His Important Teachings*. Edited by Rajiv Mehrotra. Toronto: Penguin, 2006.

———. *Ethics for the New Millennium*. New York: Riverhead Books, 1999.

———. *Freedom in Exile: The Autobiography of the Dalai Lama*. San Francisco, Calif.: HarperSanFrancisco, 1991.

———. *Healing Anger: The Power of Patience from a Buddhist Perspective*. Ithaca, N.Y.: Snow Lion Publications, 1997.

———. *The World of Tibetan Buddhism: An Overview of Its Philosophy and Practice*. Edited, translated, and annotated by Geshe Thupten Jinpa. Somerville, Mass.: Wisdom Publications, 1995.

Dass, Ram. *Grist for the Mill*. With Stephen Levine. London: Wildwood House, 1976.

Dass, Ram, and Mirabai Bush. *Compassion in Action: Setting Out on the Path of Service*. New York: Harmony/Bell Tower, 1992.

Dürckheim, Karlfried Graf. *The Way of Transformation: Daily Life as Spiritual Practice*. London: Allen & Unwin, 1988.

Epstein, Mark. *Thoughts Without a Thinker: Psychotherapy from a Buddhist Perspective*. New York: Basic Books, 1995.

Feldman, Christina. *Compassion: Listening to the Cries of the World*. Berkeley, Calif.: Rodmell Press, 2005.

Fields, Rick. "The Buddha and the Goddess" in *Dharma Gaia: A Harvest of Essays in Buddhism & Ecology*. Edited by Allan Hunt Badiner. Berkeley, Calif.: Parallax Press, 1990.

Fischer, Zoketsu Norman. "One Heart Grace." Written for Zen Hospice Project, September 1996. http://www.everydayzen.org/index.php?option=com_poetry&task=viewPoem&id=99&Itemid=28 (accessed January 27, 2010).

Gandhi, Mahatma. *Gandhi: An Autobiography: The Story of My Experiments with Truth*. Boston, Mass.: Beacon Press, 1993.

———.*Gandhi*. DVD. Written by John Briley. Directed by Richard Attenborough. Culver City, Calif.: Columbia Pictures, 1982.

Gandhi, Mohandas K. *True Patriotism: Some Sayings of Mahatma Gandhi*. Edited by S. Hobhouse. Publisher unknown.

Gendun Rinpoche, Lama. "Free and Easy." From Karma Tarchine Lundroup Buddhist Monastery, Biollet, France.

Goenka, S. N. "The Art of Living: Vipassana Meditation." A dharma talk, date unknown.

Goldberg, Natalie. *Long Quiet Highway: Waking Up in America*. New York: Bantam, 1994.

Goldstein, Joseph. *Insight Meditation: The Practice of Freedom*. Boston, Mass.: Shambhala Publications, 1993.

———. *One Dharma: The Emerging Western Buddhism*. New York: Harper One, 2003.

Goldstein, Joseph, and Jack Kornfield. *Seeking the Heart of Wisdom: The Path of Insight Meditation*. Boston, Mass.: Shambhala Publications, 1987.

Govinda, Lama Anagarika. *The Way of the White Clouds*. Woodstock, N.Y.: Overlook TP, 2006.

Hanh, Thich Nhat. *Being Peace*. Berkeley, Calif.: Parallax Press, 2006.

———. *The Miracle of Mindfulness: An Introduction to the Practice of Meditation*. Translated by Mobi Ho. Boston, Mass.: Beacon Press, 1987.

———. *No Death, No Fear: Comforting Wisdom for Life*. New York: Riverhead Books, 2002.

———. *Present Moment, Wonderful Moment: Mindfulness Verses for Daily Living*. Berkeley, Calif.: Parallax Press, 1990.

Harrison, Gavin. *In the Lap of the Buddha*. Boston, Mass.: Shambhala Publications, 1994.

Hesse, Hermann. *Siddhartha*. Translated by Hilda Rosner. New York: New Directions, 1951.

Ingram, Catherine. *Passionate Presence: Seven Qualities of Awakened Awareness*. Portland, Ore.: Diamond Books, 2008.

Kabat-Zinn, Jon. *Wherever You Go, There You Are: Mindfulness Meditation in Everyday Life*. New York: Hyperion, 1993.

Kalu Rinpoche. *The Dharma: That Illuminates All Beings Impartially Like the Light of the Sun and the Moon*. Albany, N.Y.: State University of New York Press, 1986.

Kapleau, Roshi Philip. *The Three Pillars of Zen: Teaching, Practice, and Enlightenment*. New York: Anchor Books, 1989.

Khandro Rinpoche. *This Precious Life: Buddhist Teachings on the Path to Enlightenment*. Boston, Mass.: Shambhala Publications, 2003.

Khema, Ayya. *I Give You My Life: The Autobiography of a Western Buddhist Nun*. Boston, Mass.: Shambhala Publications, 1998.

Khyentse Rinpoche, Dilgo. "Three Short Teachings" Web site article from Shechen, Dilgo Khyentse Foundation. http://www.shechen. org.tw/ec99/shop1338/english/teach_three_dkr.html (accessed January 27, 2010).

King, Martin Luther, Jr. "What Is Your Life's Blueprint?" Speech at Barratt Junior High School, Philadelphia, Pa., October 26, 1967. http://seattletimes.nwsource.com/special/mlk/king/blueprint. html (accessed January 27, 2010).

Kornfield, Jack. *A Path With Heart: A Guide through the Perils and Promises of Spiritual Life*. New York: Bantam Books, 1993.

———. *The Wise Heart: A Guide to the Universal Teachings of Buddhist Psychology*. New York: Bantam Books, 2008.

Kornfield, Jack, and Paul Breiter. *A Still Forest Pool: The Insight Meditation of Achaan Chah*. Wheaton, Ill.: Quest Publications, 1985.

Kornfield, Jack, and Christina Feldman. *Soul Food: Stories to Nourish the Spirit and the Heart*. New York: HarperOne, 1996.

Krishnamurti, J. *Freedom from the Known: A Synthesis of What Krishnamurti Has to Say about the Human Predicament and the Eternal Problems of Living*. New York: Harper & Row, 1969.

Levine, Noah. *Against the Stream: A Buddhist Manual for Spiritual Revolutionaries*. New York: HarperCollins, 2007.

Levine, Stephen. *Turning Toward the Mystery: A Seeker's Journey*. New York: HarperCollins, 2003.

Mackenzie, Vicki (Tenzin Palmo). *Cave in the Snow: Tenzin Palmo's Quest for Enlightenment*. New York: Bloomsbury USA, 1999.

Macy, Joanna. *World as Lover, World as Self*. Berkeley, Calif.: Parallax Press, 2007.

Maezumi, Taizan. *The Hazy Moon of Enlightenment*. Los Angeles: Center Publications, Zen Center of Los Angeles, 1977.

Maezumi, Taizan, and Bernie Glassman. *The Hazy Moon of Enlightenment: Part of the On Zen Practice Collection*. Somerville, Mass.: Wisdom Publications, 2007.

Maha Ghosananda. *Step by Step: Meditations on Wisdom and Compassion*. Berkeley, Calif.: Parallax Press, 1992.

Mipham, Sakyong. *Ruling Your World: Ancient Strategies for Modern Life*. New York: Doubleday, 2006.

———. *Turning the Mind into an Ally*. New York: The Berkeley Publishing Group, 2004.

Murphy, Sean. "Seventeen American Zen Stories." *The Sun* magazine, Chapel Hill, NC, October 2002.

Nisker, Wes. *Buddha's Nature: A Practical Guide to Discovering Your Place in the Cosmos*. New York: Bantam Books, 2000.

Nyanaponika Thera. *The Heart of Buddhist Meditation*. Newburyport, Mass.: Weiser Books, 1973.

Oxenhandler, Noelle. "Where Does It End?" *Tricycle,* Fall 2001.

Packer, Toni. *The Work of This Moment*. Boston, Mass.: Shambhala Publications, 2007.

Salzberg, Sharon. *Faith: Trusting Your Own Deepest Experience*. New York: Riverhead, 2002.

———. *Lovingkindness: The Revolutionary Art of Happiness*. Boston, Mass.: Shambhala Publications, 2002.

Schmidt, Amy. *Knee Deep in Grace: The Extraordinary Life and Teaching of Dipa Ma*. Lake Junaluska, N.C.: Present Perfect Books, 2002.

Schumacher, E. F. *Small Is Beautiful: Economics as if People Mattered*. New York: Harper & Row, 1973.

Snyder, Gary. *Left Out in the Rain: Poems*. Berkeley, Calif.: Counterpoint, 2005.

———. *Myths & Texts*. New York: New Directions, 1978.

Sogyal Rinpoche. *The Tibetan Book of Living and Dying*. San Francisco, Calif.: HarperSanFrancisco, 1992.

Sumedho, Ajahn. *Cittaviveka Teachings from the Silent Mind*. Hertfordshire, U.K.: Amarvati Publications, 1987.

———. *The Way It Is*. Hertfordshire, U.K.: Amarvati Publications, 1991.

Surya Das, Lama. *Awakening the Buddha Within: Tibetan Wisdom for the Western World*. New York: Broadway Books, 1997.

Suzuki, Shunryu. *Zen Mind, Beginner's Mind*. Boston, Mass.: Weath-erhill, 1973.

Thondup, Tulku. *The Healing Power of Mind: Simple Meditation Exercises for Health, Well-Being, and Enlightenment*. Boston, Mass.: Shambhala Publications, 1996.

Thurman, Robert. *Inner Revolution: Life, Liberty, and the Pursuit of Real Happiness*. New York: Riverhead Books, 1999.

Trungpa, Chögyam. *Cutting Through Spiritual Materialism.* Boston, Mass.: Shambhala Publications, 1974.

———. *The Myth of Freedom and the Way of Meditation*. Boston, Mass.: Shambhala Publications, 2002.

———. *Shambhala: The Sacred Path of the Warrior*. Boston, Mass.: Shambhala Publications, 1988.

Wallace, B. Alan. *Tibetan Buddhism from the Ground Up: A Practical Approach for Modern Life*. Boston, Mass.: Wisdom Publications, 1993.

Watts, Alan. *The Way of Zen*. New York: Vintage, 1999.

———. *The Wisdom of Insecurity: A Message for an Age of Anxiety*. New York: Pantheon, 1968.

Winston, Diana. *Wide Awake: A Buddhist Guide for Teens*. New York: Perigree, 2003.

Yen, Sheng. *Faith in Mind: A Commentary on Seng Ts'an's Classic*. Boston, Mass.: Shambhala Publications, 2006.

———. *The Method of No-Method: The Chan Practice of Silent Illumina-tion*. Boston: Shambhala Publications, 2008.

Yeshe, Lama. *Becoming Your Own Therapist and Making Your Mind an Ocean*. Edited by Nicholas Ribush. Boston, Mass.: Lama Yeshe Wisdom Archive, 2006.

CREDITS

INDEX OF TEACHERS

ABOUT THE EDITORS

Jack Kornfield trained as a Buddhist monk in the monasteries of Thailand, India, and Burma. He has taught meditation internationally since 1974 and is one of the key teachers to introduce Buddhist mindfulness practice to the West. He is a founding teacher of the Insight Meditation Society and Spirit Rock Meditation Center. He holds a PhD in clinical psychology, is the author of many books, and is a husband and father. For more information on Jack Kornfield's teachings, visit www.jackkornfield.org.

Noelle Oxenhandler is the author of two nonfiction books, *A Grief Out of Season* and *The Eros of Parenthood*. Her essays have appeared in many national and literary magazines, including *The New Yorker, The New York Times Magazine, Vogue, Tricycle,* and *O: The Oprah Magazine.* She is a member of the creative writing faculty at Sonoma State University in California. A practicing Buddhist for more than thirty years, Oxenhandler is the mother of a grown daughter and lives in Northern California. For more information, visit www.noelleoxenhandler.com.

For more information about Buddhist practice and mindfulness teachings, visit:

Spirit Rock Meditation Center
5000 Sir Francis Drake Blvd.
Woodacre, CA 94973
415-488-0164
www.spiritrock.org

Insight Meditation Society
1230 Pleasant Street
Barre, MA 01005
978-355-4378
www.dharma.org

Jack Kornfield
www.jackkornfield.org

Additional meditations available for free online at www.shambhala. com/stillteaching: "The Practice of Zazen" by Pat Enkyo O'Hara; "Insight Meditation" by Mahasi Sayadaw; "The Practice of Loving-kindness (Metta)" by Sharon Salzberg; "The Practice of Tonglen" by Pema Chödrön; "Feeding the Demons" by Tsultrim Allione; "Forgiveness Meditation" by Jack Kornfield.

Library of Congress Cataloging-in-Publication Data

The Buddha is still teaching: contemporary Buddhist wisdom/
selected and edited by Jack Kornfield with Noelle Oxenhandler.—
1st ed.
p. cm.
ISBN 978-1-59030-692-5 (hardcover: alk. paper)
1. Spiritual life—Buddhism. 2. Buddhism—Doctrines.
I. Kornfield, Jack, 1945–
II. Oxenhandler, Noelle, 1952–
BQ4302.B83 2011
294.3'444—dc22
2010024323